# THE *SAVVY* GUIDE TO BUYING COLLECTOR CARS AT AUCTION

# THE *SAVVY* GUIDE TO BUYING COLLECTOR CARS AT AUCTION

JAMES C. MAYS

INDIANAPOLIS

Indy-Tech Publishing is an imprint of Sams Technical Publishing, LLC, 9850 East 30th Street, Indianapolis, Indiana 46229.



International Standard Book Number: 0-7906-1322-0



Chief Executive Officer: Alan Symons
President: Scott Weaver
Chief Financial Officer: Keith Siergiej
Chief Operating Officer: Richard White
Acquisitions Editor: Brad Schepp
Editorial Assistant: Dana Eaton
Copy Editor: Beth Price
Pagination Editor: Kim Heusel
Cover Design: Mike Walsh
Technical Editor: Jim Lenzke
Photos: RM Auctions, Inc., Barrett-Jackson Auction Company, Larry Finley Auctioneers & Appraisers, Kruse International, Craig and Alane Grosz, Tom and Kathy Truhar, Spanky (Tommy) and Amy Assiter, Jim Cox, Branson Auto Auctions, Inc., Elton McFall, Jim Heide, David Hansen, Cox Auctions, Rob Myers, James Mays



Manufactured in the USA

# CONTENTS

# PREFACE

An auction is one of the most unforgettable venues in which one can buy a vintage vehicle. Thrilling and memorable experiences, auctions take place in a public forum where every eye in the house is on the bidders. In short, the purchasers provide entertainment and drama amongst themselves and to the non-bidding audience as well. Don't be intimidated because you aren't familiar with the rules, the etiquette, or the lingo that defines the experience.

At an auction, buyers and sellers come together in a special environment for mutual benefit. Webster notes the word "auction" entered into the English language officially in 1595 with the definition, "to sell property to the highest bidder." Auction traces its heritage from the Latin word *auctio,* meaning, "to increase."

The price is not the only thing that increases at an auction, so does the pleasure of a very unique kind of shopping while hobnobbing with buddies and chasing your dream wheels.

You hold in your hands a step-by-step guide designed to educate the first-timer on the complete collector vehicle auction process. You will learn exactly how a collectible vehicle is purchased at a public auction. This book lays out the knowledge and understanding needed to make the auction a positive experience, one you will be wise and eager to repeat.

Auctions are lightening-paced, and you need to be aware of what happens, when it happens, and how it happens. Here you will learn the many practical "do's" and "don'ts" that will ultimately reward you with ownership of your dream vehicle.

To bring you the most valuable information there is, I consulted with a number of the major vintage car auction houses. I talked with auctioneers, auction staff, consumers, and critics, too. Each person interviewed offers a unique and important perspective to the overall process. In gathering these facts and tips together in one handy, easy-to-read, and easy-to-understand guide, this tool is designed to give a satisfying consumer experience in the electrically charged atmosphere of the vintage automobile auction world.

You will learn to define your collector desires and to refine your needs so your investment fits comfortably into your lifestyle. You will learn to find the right vehicle and to estimate its value and authenticity. You will become acquainted with the many different types of auctions and the processes inherent with each kind. Common pitfalls and scams are identified. Consumer rights and laws are covered, too. Finally, you will have a better understanding of how to enjoy your wheels once the auctioneer's gavel falls.

It is my sincere wish that you enjoy hunting and finding your special vehicle, that you shop wisely, and that the auction experience is one that will keep you coming back time and time again.

James C. Mays
Windsor, Ontario

## Acknowledgments

I wish to thank my colleagues, especially historian Patrick Foster. Without his encouragement, I would never have started writing automotive histories. Mary Baruth, the City of Windsor's heritage and culture development advisor, offers invaluable insights. Jan and Murray McEwan at *Old Autos* deserve special thanks for taking a chance on an unknown writer as well as Keith Mathiowetz and Angelo Van Bogart at *Old Cars*. Patrick Ertel at *Vintage Truck* and *Antique Power* stretches my limits in new fields as does Merry Dudley at *Toy Cars & Models*, Dave Hunter and Mark Long at *The Drive*, and Chad Elmore, managing editor of *OEM Off-Highway* and *Belt Pulley.*

Then, I want to thank my agent Matt Wagner for the gig, the editorial team at Indy-Tech, Dana Eaton and Brad Schepp, as well as my technical editor, Jim Lenzke, for their guidance and suggestions that shaped this book.

I would be remiss if I did not thank the following individuals for their generous time in interviews and research assistance: Spanky and Amy Assiter; Joe Belland at the Auctioneers Association of Canada; Brian Carlson at *Old Cars;* Jim Cox at Cox Auctions; Larry Finley at Larry

Finley Auctioneers & Appraisers; Craig Grosz; David Hanson; Craig Jackson, Ginger Wilber, Jill Smith, and Gary Bennett at Barrett-Jackson; Dean Kruse at Kruse International; Bertrand Lauzon; Rob Myers and Terry Lobzun at RM Auctions, Inc.; and Tom and Kathy Truhlar at Kent's Big Bar.

Then there are my friends and family, the true believers who stick with me through thick and thin and believe that every new book is better than the last. Thanks to Howard Belsky and Glenn Burt, Kevin Casey, Reid and Margaret Coolen, Martha Daniels and Diane Knaus, Rob DeKort and Deborah MacVicar, Kevin Demers, Alice D'Odean, Chad and Katie Elmore, Lila Gottheil, Lois Graham, Nicole Green, Randy Green, Lee and Michelle Hastings, Robyn Hayle, Dave and Clare Ivany, Jason Ives and Catherine McIntosh, Anne Jared, Gerry and Mark Lehman, Paul Lehman, the Myke Leonard family, Nathalie Maillet, Margaret Marshall and Charmaine LaForest, Amy Maycock, Gordon Mays and Theresa Pittman, Wayne and Becky Mays, Elizabeth Miller, Terry and Bonnie Noble, John and Dot Oakes, John Oakes, Dorothy Jean Perkins, the Don Plenderleith family, Beverly Reeves, Vince Ruffolo and Carol Capelle, Andres Runnels, Rob Saunders, Dominic Sauve, Doug Schapiro and Nancy Michaud, John Shellhorn and AJ Stead, Carole Shepard, Craig Shoemaker, Dick and Lely Tucker, Olivier Vendette, and Robert Vock.

Finally, a *gros merci* goes to Francois Pigeon who is not only a dear friend but also the very best mechanic in the world!

James Mays
Windsor, Ontario

# INTRODUCTION

## In the Beginning

Like every other collectible hobby, vintage automobile ownership is driven first by nostalgia and then by desirability as an investment. You will have to decide if you are buying a set of wheels to put on the road for enjoyment or a prized collectible that will be carefully stored while it rises in value. You will have to determine if this is a "feel good," ego-satisfying, extension-of-your-personality purchase or a dream vehicle that represents a cold, calculated hedge against the uncertainties of the future. Before you make any decisions, you will benefit by knowing something about the history of car collecting in order to put your thoughts into perspective.

The old car hobby first surfaced in North America in an appreciable, organized way during the 1930s as interest grew around the Brass Era cars. In danger of disappearing in the Dirty Thirties, dealers crushed countless old cars built before 1915. Acting on behalf of manufacturers, the authorized destruction of older cars was a bold and calculated bid to dry up the used car market and sell new vehicles, thus stimulating a very troubled economy. Dealers were paid $25 for each old car taken in on trade and then certified as wrecked. I personally know of several quarries in New England where dealers are said to have sent hundreds of vintage vehicles to their final resting place. The manufacturers weren't very successful with the program, by the way.

If the Great Depression wasn't enough to endanger their existence, tens of thousands of older vehicles were recycled into sorely needed weapons and placed in the hands of soldiers, fighting for victory during World War II. Folks cheerfully turned over the rusted Autocar, Brush, Chalmers, and countless other vehicles to those collecting metal for scrap drives. Better on the battlefront than in the backyard was the reasoning.

## Clubs Begin to Organize

Fearing that automotive history was about to disappear right in front of their very eyes, people who cared banded together to form organizations with the goal of preserving the remaining remnant of these once beautiful horseless carriages. The most enduring organization is the Antique Automobile Club of America, founded in 1935. This group limited its interest to the Brass Era cars, called so because of the large amount of brass ornamentation used on them. The practice ended—along with the era—in 1915.

The automotive industry marked its Golden Jubilee in 1946, sparking a widespread interest in older cars. The Classic Car Club of America was founded in 1952 to honor the limited edition, expensive, "fine," and "distinctive" automobiles built between 1925 and 1948. These magnificent machines included such grand marques as Pierce-Arrow, Packard, Peerless, Auburn, Cord, Duesenberg, Cadillac, and Lincoln. European cars are included as well. Their distinguishing hallmarks are an initial high price in the luxury market and custom coachwork. Though there are exceptions, virtually all of these vehicles were built between 1925 and 1948.

These hand-built confections with their custom coachwork, beveled crystal glass windows, and those genuine leopard-skin interiors, by the way, are the only vehicles designated as classic cars. Don't ever let anyone tell you that a 1957 Chevrolet or a 1955 Ford Thunderbird is a classic. They aren't. They are vintage, collectible, milestone or collector cars, but they do not meet the criteria laid down by the Classic Car Club of America to qualify as a *bona fide* Classic.

The Milestone Car Society sets the definition for notable automobiles built from 1945 through 1972. The list includes many post-war favorites like the 1957 Chevrolet and not so well-known vehicles like the 1951 Kaiser Golden Dragon.

Clubs specific to marques followed slowly in the wake of the 1946 Golden Jubilee. Hardy Volkswagen lovers banded together in 1955. The Pierce-Arrow Society was created in 1957 to preserve that prestigious automobile's heritage. Hudson, Essex, and Terraplane buffs founded a national organization in 1959, only two years after Hudson was sent to that great scrapyard in the sky. The National Council of Corvette Clubs was formed the same year to preserve and promote Chevrolet's sports car. The unique Art Deco Chrysler Airflows of the 1930s got a club in 1962. The Antique and Classic Car Club of Canada was formally chartered in 1963. Fans of Studebaker and Oldsmobile founded respective clubs in 1971. Proliferating throughout the seventies, today there is a club for virtually every kind of vehicle ever built from AMC's Pacer to the glittering Duesenberg.

### Replicars and Kit Cars

While these are not historically accurate examples of manufactured vehicles, kit cars and replicars often turn up at auctions. They are legitimate genres of collectible vehicles in their own right and have a large, faithful following. Kit cars are build-it-yourself vehicles and encompass a large group of rolling stock including dune buggies, the Devon, Astra, the CalSpyder, Manx, and numerous Cobra wannabes.

Some cars are a marriage of an updated classic look based on modern chassis. Designed strictly for pleasure, they include the Diamante, the Zimmer, the Johnson, and the Panther Westwinds. While purists discretely disdain these Johnny-come-latelys, they command a strong presence at collector car auctions.

Replicars are modern updates of timeless classics. Having stood the test of time, these vehicles have become classics in their own right. They include such distinguished nameplates as Auburn, Cord, the Excalibur, Timmins, and Duesenberg II.

### Custom Cars

Vehicles that have been modified are very often seen at auctions. Modifications might include a different engine—usually bigger—and, on older models, smaller wheels. Special paint jobs are often incorporated. This becomes a custom car when the chassis is lowered, the roof is "chopped," door handles are "shaved," and other appearance changes are made. The taillights from a 1956 Packard might be grafted onto the rear of a 1949 Mercury. Custom cars often look nothing like the original models.

### Hot Rods

Hot rods are two-seaters. Little or no attempt is made to disguise their origins. There are four categories of hot rods. Hardcore rods are the classics, recreating the earliest days of the rodding hobby. They feature exposed engines. Traditional rods look like those early machines but incorporate modern parts and the latest technology. Street rods use modern parts and are designed for comfort as well as race capacity. Finally, there are the show rods, spectacular creations designed to dazzle and delight the eye.

Barrett-Jackson has an exclusive arrangement to sell the confections of Chip Foose, who stars in The Learning Channel's show *Overhaulin'*, and Boyd Coddington's creations showcased on *American Hot Rod* on the Discovery Channel.

## Specialty Cars

Specialty cars include those made from scratch or customized for television or the movies. Some of the best-known ones include the Batmobile, the Green Hornet's car, and the Munsters' car.

## Concept Cars

These beauties are truly rare because they are one-off show cars built by the manufacturer, usually to get opinions from the public about where styling might go in the future. When concept cars do cross the block, they cost a king's ransom. The 1954 Oldsmobile F-88 show car built by GM sold at the Barrett-Jackson auction for more than $3 million in 2005.

## Race Cars

Official competition cars cross the block from time to time. These racetrack heroes are certified and authenticated as being the real McCoy, and they sell just as fast as they tear around the track. When purchasing a genuine racer, the owner will be required to sign a disclaimer that the vehicle is not authorized for ordinary road use.

Gary Bennett, the senior automotive specialist at Barrett-Jackson, is a collector who is serious about speed and owned the 1970 Trans-Am class Chevrolet Camaro raced by Ron Kirby. Kirby and his Camaro competed against such legends as Mark Donohue in his AMC Javelin, George Follmer and Parnelli Jones in their Ford Mustangs, and Dan Gurney in his AAR Plymouth Barracuda. Gary put the Camaro in the auction without reserve. The hammer came down on the Trans-Am racer at $100,000, and he was satisfied that it was the best price that he would ever get for the car.

## The Hobby Mushrooms

Older vehicles have always been restored and traded hands. By the middle of the 1950s, the hobby had become common enough that most states and provinces designated cars 25 years and older as antiques. Special regulations governing their use were enacted, and discounts on plates and registrations were put into place. Insurance companies followed suit with special categories for these veterans of the road. Prices of vintage vehicles rose steadily throughout the 1960s simply because of the law of supply and demand. There were far more would-be collectors than there were old wheels available to collectors.

Clubs quickly expanded their focus to be much more than a source of information and a clearinghouse for parts; they began to provide events where owners might showcase their rescued beauties and permit the public to enjoy them, as well. Some of these clubs have experienced incredible support and have grown to include museums and extensive libraries and to sponsor on-site flea markets, banquets, dances, and guest speakers. With time, manufacturers, museums, old car publications, even municipalities have gotten in on the act of throwing events to pay homage to collectible cars.

*Hemmings Motor News* appeared on the market for the first time in January of 1954 as an antique cars and parts guide. It grew to include current values and was joined in 1987 by the annual *Standard Guide to Cars & Prices,* published by Krause. *The NADA Price Guide* and the *Sanford Evans Gold Book* have offered antique car value guides for many years. The latter two publications are better known inside the trade than to hobbyists.

## Auction History

The very first auction to feature only used (not collectible) automobiles was in 1938. Held by Rawl's Auto Auction in Leesville, South Carolina, it was a modest beginning. Barrett-Jackson began auctioning off collectible vehicles in 1971 with its first event in Scottsdale, Arizona. That same year, Kruse International began selling vintage automobiles as well in Auburn, Indiana. RM Auctions, Inc., based in Blenheim, Ontario, broadened its base from restoration to auction galas in 1979.

Today, the old car hobby has mushroomed into a full-fledged industry, employing nearly a million people in North America alone. These workers remanufacture scarce or obsolete parts, restore entire vehicles, research their histories, sell and service these beautiful machines, and maintain museums and important archives. Some are historians, writing informative articles for newspapers, magazines, and even books like this.

The National Auctioneers Association underwrote two studies in 2003 in order to get an accurate picture of the industry. The first study showed that auctions currently generate $200 billion a year and enjoy a growth rate of 4 percent annually. Of that $200 billion, automotive auctions are by far the largest segment, capturing 42 percent of the market.

Auctions are highly social events, places where people relax and spend time with friends. A man who usually spent his leisure time in Las Vegas at the gambling tables decided to check out the Barrett-Jackson event. He had a good enough time that the next year he returned with a private jet and six of his friends. The word got around and the following year, six jets filled with his friends arrived in Scottsdale, Arizona. One of the men invited his lawyer to tag along, and the counselor went home with three cars that cost him $400,000.

A whopping 92 percent of all Americans have attended at least one live auction, and roughly 8 percent takes part in auctions at least once a year, often online. The most highly attended auctions are "high-end" glamour events and those where the profits are earmarked for charities.

Since the tragedy of September 11, many people have stopped putting off their dreams and begun to live them. Craig Jackson, president and CEO of collector car giant Barrett-Jackson Inc., recalls that for a week after that horrible day the phones in his office were silent. Then the phone rang. A Wall Street broker called to say, "I lost a lot of friends last week. I have always wanted to come to Scottsdale, and now I am going to do it and bring my kids." True to his word, he did come and brought his children. The broker went home with his dream wheels, a Shelby GT 500.

## Automobiles Are Our Heritage

Every person who participates in the old car hobby is doing something to preserve an important part of our legacy and culture. Each vehicle restored is another chapter of history that might otherwise be lost. The story of the twentieth century in North America is essentially that of the automobile. It is the most desirable artifact of our culture. Each automobile rescued and restored is more than history; it is also a work of art. How easy it is to teach history and instill pride in the generations that follow in our footsteps when the lesson is wrapped in something as cool as a collectible vehicle!

Auctions play an important part in bringing automotive history to a public that might otherwise be too busy to search for these vehicles on its own. Auction events provide a unique venue where buyers can make a purchase in an extremely limited time frame with minimum fuss.

With these thumbnail sketches of automobile history, car club history, and automobile auction history, you can now move forward with understanding. Happy bidding!

# About the Author

Family folklore has it that James Mays' first word was not "mama" or "dada." It was "Buick." His mouth was immediately washed out with soap because he was born into the home of respectable Nash people. The kid learned to drive on the family's JI Case tractor and grew up passionately loving all four-wheeled vehicles. He admits to being partial to American Motors products.

Mays is a graduate of Andrews University in Michigan and Concordia University in Montreal. A meticulous researcher, he writes with insight and humor. The award-winning author has 30 books to his credit, including five cookbooks and six automotive histories.

A respected authority on collectible cars, trucks, and tractors, Mays writes more than 300 articles a year. He contributes to *V-8, Toy Cars & Models, Reader's Digest, OEM PowerSports, OEM Off-Highway*, and *Automobile Quarterly*. His columns appear regularly in *Old Autos*, Canada's newspaper for the enthusiast, and *Old Cars*. He is a staff writer for *Vintage Truck, Antique Power,* and *Belt Pulley*.

A member of the Society of Automotive Historians and the Canadian Automotive Historians Association, Mays lives in Windsor, Ontario, Canada's Motor City. Keenly interested in Windsor's history, Mays writes historical columns for *Scoop* and *The Drive*. He is heard frequently on CBC Radio One. A permanent collection of his works is housed at the University of Windsor's Leddy Library in the James Mays Collection.

Other automotive books by the author:

- *Rescued & Restored: Canadians and their Collectable Cars*
- *The American Motors Century*
- *Rambler Canada: The Little Company that Could*
- *Ford and Canada: 100 Years Together*
- *From Kenosha to the World: The Rambler, Jeffery and Nash Truck Story*
- *Ford Ranchero: 1957-1979 Photo History*

# Dedication

To Bonnie J. Johnson, my Grade Nine English teacher, whose love of language inspired me to become a writer.

# 1 CASHING IN WISELY ON NOSTALGIA

## VEHICLE SELECTION AND FAMILY CONSIDERATION

The very first step you will take is to determine whether or not a collector car fits your lifestyle. The notion of owning a vintage set of wheels is romantic, but like puppies, it requires a great deal of time and attention. Sit down, clear some space off your dusty, cluttered desk, and make a list of times in a season you will actually get behind the wheel of your dream car and cruise off into the sunset. Use the calendar and be brutally realistic. Pencil in dates.

Unless you live in the most temperate of climates, you are most likely to use your car primarily between April or May through September or October. That is a maximum of six months' enjoyment. Folks who live in the southern part of the continent or on the West Coast will enjoy longer seasons, commensurate with milder weather patterns. Remember, climate is king. Plan accordingly!

# Make Sure a Collectible Car Suits Your Lifestyle

Most of us are so caught up in the daily grind we barely have time to squeeze in life's basics. Another 24-hour period slips by, and we have not accomplished half of what we set out to do for the day. That urgent, unfinished business gets piled on top of tomorrow's already jammed agenda. We juggle carpooling responsibilities and hustle the kids to hockey practice, Japanese lessons, and piano recitals. Appointments with the dentist, the doctor, and the accountant as well as visits with the parents and the in-laws are important and somehow get squeezed into the day. Hurried and harried, we fall behind quickly. We bring our work home with us and burn midnight oil. Life is precarious. There is no time for accidents or disasters. The frenetic pace we set leaves us gasping, with very little quality time for our hobbies and ourselves. No wonder we need to book time with the therapist on Tuesdays at four!

Oh, sure, you are the first to admit that the idea of dropping the top on that '65 Plymouth Fury III and taking a spin into the countryside to pick apples sounds tempting. Then reality sets in. The lawn is in desperate need of mowing. The grass is so tall there may already be a pride of lions hiding in it. Before that jungle can be mowed, the blades need to be taken off the lawn tractor and sharpened. Since the grinder is broken, that means a trip to the garage. Then, there is the downstairs toilet; it's leaking, again. There are at least six other items that your significant other has placed on the "urgent list" that need to be taken care of immediately if you expect escape with your life until next Tuesday. So, you sigh and forget about the planned escape in the Plymouth. The Fury III will have to wait patiently for another week and the apples ... well, there will be another crop of Northern Spies next year.

The 1966 Plymouth Fury is a satisfying ride for MoPar collectors who want speed and comfort.

If you can't carve out enough time to give yourself at least a 15 percent usage rate during the season, this collectible car venture may prove to be far more expensive than fun. An older car demands attention. If it isn't driven, seals dry out and the rubber rots. Upholstery can be ruined while the car sits in long-term storage, and as sure as it snows in Chicago in December, engine trouble will develop if the vehicle is left sitting unattended for long periods of time. If you don't have time to look after it, your wheels will depreciate in value, right under your nose. You can't be sentenced to prison for car neglect, but your conscience will guilt trip you often enough as you watch your prize wheels deteriorate.

Savvy Tip

You should be able to give yourself a minimum of four weekends out of the old car season for the enjoyment of your dream wheels. If you can't, you are not a good candidate to own a collectible car. You should not own a collectible vehicle if you are only going to spend time maintaining a car you don't ever get to enjoy.

## Your Collectible Car May Be a Business Expense

There is no need to raise a quizzical eyebrow at the thought. The instant your car is connected to your business in some meaningful way, it is a definite expense and therefore legitimately tax deductible. Put that vintage 'Vette to use in promoting the business. You might choose to use it in an advertising campaign or in the field as a promotional tool. You will need an accountant's expertise to tell you exactly what the limitations are and how much of a deduction you are entitled to, but the old girl will be doing her part to earn her keep while you turn heads on the highways!

## Consider a Working Girl

If you are at all adventurous with your entrepreneurial skills, you may find a way to build an entire line of work or even a lifestyle around your collectible car purchase. Bertrand Lauzon of Montreal discovered a one-owner, 1960 DeSoto stashed in a garage. The magnificent car, with

The 1958 Edsel is more popular today then when it was new, an exception to the general rule. Be prepared to spend up to $30,000 for a Corsair in Number One condition.

its elegant lines and soaring fins, was like new. It had belonged to a milkman who only drove it on weekends. The milkman died, and his wife never moved it from its parking spot. This delightful, de-lovely DeSoto dream had very few miles on the odometer and needed only the most minor of attention to bring it up to snuff.

The new owner didn't need a DeSoto any more than he needed a hole drilled into his head. He was an extremely busy man. In fact, his days were so packed, he worried that this was a foolish purchase. He would never find the time to kick back and enjoy the car.

Those startling, troubling thoughts prompted Bertrand to reflect seriously about what he wanted out of life. As he struggled to find time to play with the DeSoto, he began to idly tinker with the idea of quitting his job. The exercise grew into a list of possibilities of different, new lifestyles, each one centered on including quality time with his dream wheels. A longtime reporter for a daily newspaper in the city, the man decided he was ready for a major change. He gave notice to his employer and took the plunge into a completely new line of work.

Bertrand bought a period trailer that looked just right in tandem with the DeSoto. Outfitting the trailer fully with all the amenities found in a mobile or field office, the old girl was hitched to the smart little tagalong. The pair appeared at huge events where the owner rented out the office space to members of the media needing a place to write and file stories with their editors. In short order the DeSoto owner was highly contented with his new, very relaxed lifestyle and after years of sitting in storage, the DeSoto became a "working girl," earning a substantial income.

Tom and Kathy Truhlar of Fort Atkinson, Wisconsin, had the same idea. They make and sell homemade ice cream bars at antique car, truck, and tractor shows in the Midwest. At least half the fun of buying a Kent's Big Bar is lining up in front of the beautiful, fully restored, pale green, 1953 Chevrolet Step Van, their rightful pride and joy. The vintage van has been such a hit with the public that they now have plans in place to restore a 1961 International C-130 pickup truck and put it to work, too.

## You Are What You Drive

Whether you want to be seen behind the wheel of a Rolls-Royce, a Volkswagen Beetle, a Yugo, or a Lada, the vehicle you drive speaks volumes about you. Owning an antique car brings you instant acceptability into the old car world. You can love Corvettes with all your heart and soul and even join a club. But, until you take the plunge and bolt the plate onto a real one, your passion is only theoretical.

It is always surprising how often cars match their owners' personalities. A man I knew owns a 1977 Dodge Colt. It has a toothy grin, and so did he. Cars have personalities of their own. Collectible vehicles often acquire monikers. My mother was always of the opinion that cars and trucks were like pets; they needed names. "It's not nice to leave your car unnamed. If you don't name it, it won't give you good gas mileage," she always warned. Heeding her wisdom, every vehicle I have ever known has been duly christened. My Frost White 1969 AMC Ambassador wagon was "Blanche." I drove it every day—year round—for a decade. Blanche became part of my persona over the years. People who couldn't remember my name had no problem recalling the unique car I drove. I have been called Blanche many times!

The 1969 Rambler SC/Rambler was a limited edition pocket rocket built by American Motors to commemorate the end of the Rambler line. It promised to make life miserable for any GTO, Roadrunner, Cobra Jet, or Mach 1. The SC/Rambler has sold for nearly $20,000 at auctions.

## Buy a Lifestyle

Craig Jackson, of Barrett-Jackson fame, says, "Car collecting is not just about buying a car, it is a lifestyle. The 'good ole boys' used to get together to share the passion of car collecting but that has all changed." Buying a car can be a life-defining moment. To illustrate his point, he shares this story.

A World War II veteran attending the Barrett-Jackson event in Scottsdale, Arizona, with his wife was introduced to Steve Davis, Jackson's right hand man. Steve recalled that the first timer had just retired from his job and the gentleman was so excited to be in Scottsdale he was literally shaking. He wanted to experience everything at the show and soak it all up. Steve gave him the big tour. A week later at the auction, Steve felt a tug, turned around, and the vet excitedly told him he had bought his dream wheels, a Thunderbird. If that wasn't enough, a half dozen of his war buddies back home had seen him by the big 'Bird on Speed magazine. It was hands down the most exciting moment of his life. The vet and the army buddies still get together every year to reminisce, and you can bet your bottom dollar what car gets driven to their annual gathering.

## Star Cars

My friend Olivier Vendette bought a 1976 AMC Pacer for $1,500 because he was just crazy about those sexy lines. The savvy 22-year old mechanic promptly registered it for movie work. To his surprise the Pacer was promptly picked up to be the "star car" for two major Hollywood movies, *Confessions of a Dangerous Mind* and *The Human Stain*. The money earned in front of the cameras far more than covered the initial purchase.

**Savvy Tip**

If your vintage vehicle can be directly linked to your business, it is a legitimate tax deduction. An accountant will advise you as to what percentage of the purchase, repairs, and upkeep can be written off to the business. Be aware that as a working girl, it may not qualify for any of the heritage insurance plans.

Few vintage cars from the '60s turn heads as fast as a 1965 Buick Riviera Gran Sport.

## Make Sure the Car Meets Your Desires

If tooling around town in a 1940 Buick Roadmaster makes you happy because Uncle Owen owned one, then, by gum that is a perfectly legitimate reason to want one. If a 1931 Cadillac does it for you then go for it! Don't let anyone try to convince you otherwise. There are few things more disquieting than learning that the lovely 1954 Mercury M-350 Express pickup truck on display was an unhappy second choice when a 1959 Dodge Sweptside hauler was the vehicle truly desired. The whole purpose of collecting anything is the feeling of satisfaction derived from the acquisition. Whether it is a Barracuda or a boat-tailed Riviera, a Falcon or a Franklin, the number one reason for purchasing a collectible car is because it brings the opportunity to experience joyful moments and the pleasure of reliving many happy memories.

The Buick Roadmaster was one of just 26 models offered in 1940.

Don't ever buy a set of wheels simply because it is a bargain; I can guarantee that nine times out of 10 you won't enjoy your purchase. A woman called one day to tell me about her 1967 Rambler Rebel Briarcliff. She bought this station wagon on a whim at an estate sale for $200. Not only was the Rambler a very striking vehicle, it was dirt-cheap. While driving it home, the new owner discovered she didn't actually like piloting a station wagon.

She had no idea that only 400 Briarcliffs were ever built or that she had taken possession of a vehicle that became a collectible before its time. The Rambler was parked in an underground garage where it sat, unloved, for decades. When I laid eyes on it, the poor thing was barely visible under 29 years' worth of dust and was packed to the gills with canning jars. I was able to introduce her to a buyer. She was as glad to be shed of the Rambler as the new owner was ecstatic with his dream find.

American Motors was awash in red ink in 1967, and the press openly predicted that the last of the independent automakers would soon declare bankruptcy and disappear. To spur interest in its products and generate sales, three limited-edition Rambler Rebel station wagons were produced. A total of 600 Mariners were finished in Barbados Blue and kissed with bleached woodgrain-like trim then trimmed off with nautically themed interiors. These were sold on the East Coast and the West Coast. The Briarcliff was painted Matador Red and given black, camera-grain side trim. Only 400 were built, and these were sold in Nashville, the northeastern states, and the Middle Atlantic states. To complete the trio, 550 Westerners were dressed in a cowboy and ranch theme for sale in the southwestern states. The aggressive program was a success and did much to help the public regain confidence in the feisty independent carmaker.

Don't buy a car simply because it's available. That's like polishing off the potato salad because there's still some left in the bowl! A friend wanted to unload his 1976 TR-7 in the worst way in order to please his wife, who hated the car. He had me take it for a spin several times. I even drove it to Boston and back. It was a nice enough vehicle, but somehow, it didn't speak to my soul. Not wishing to damage our friendship, reluctantly I turned him down, flat. I am glad I did. He sold the TR-7 to someone else, and our friendship stayed intact.

The 1975 Triumph TR-7 was not a good seller when new.

Savvy Tip

If you don't feel passionate about a vehicle, let it pass, no matter how reasonable the price. The only exception to this rule is if you know you can flip it to somebody else and not be stuck with it. There's absolutely no point to owning a vintage car or truck if the vehicle doesn't inspire you to sit up and sing.

## Try One On for Size

If the car you crave is intended for personal pleasure, don't merely dream about it; get off your duff and do something practical about it. Start by strategically placing pictures or scale models of your dream car where you can be reminded of it often. Visualize it. Make those dream wheels your screensaver on the computer. Place a jar under the picture and drop your change into it every night. All of these cues will serve to remind you of your goal and what you are going to do in order to achieve it.

Find an example of your dream car and go kick its tires. Get behind the wheel and take it for a spin. Scour the want ads and go check out a different vehicle every weekend.

For years, I dreamt of owning a Nash Metropolitan. My grandmother had owned one of these adorable Anglo-American hybrids, and as a child, I always got a thrill from riding in it. The first and only time I ever drove one of the cute little buggers, I found it far too cramped to enjoy. After my trial run, I handed the keys back to the owner and walked away. I was satisfied that I had finally driven one and was forever cured of my hunger to own a Met. Memories of Grandmother's Met will be enough for me!

The Metropolitan was built exclusively for Nash by Austin in the UK and sold in North America as a captive import beginning in 1954. It was added to the Hudson line in 1955 after Nash and Hudson merged. Rambler dealers offered the tiny cutie from 1958 to 1962. A 1961 Met is shown here.

Use common sense as your guide. No matter how desirable, a four-speed, standard transmission Oldsmobile 4-4-2 with a genuine Hurst Shifter isn't going to see a lot of asphalt if an old football injury flares up and leaves you limping after a Sunday drive to Lansing. Similarly, a 300-pound man isn't going to find it pleasant to heave his considerable girth in and out of that sleek, low-slung Bricklin. Aside from being painful, it isn't the least bit dignified. There will be plenty of laughter from onlookers—all of it at the hapless owner's expense.

## Keep an Open Mind

With pencil and paper in hand, write down a fairly broad list that encompasses a range of acceptable vehicles that you would like to explore in order to make your dream come true. Once again, be very practical in your considerations. Your family of five will be furious when you can't take them all for ice cream in your 1958 two-seater Corvette. You, on the other hand, might not get much, if any, satisfaction from driving a 1958 Chevrolet station wagon to Frosty King. Sure, the wagon wears the exact same blue bowtie as the Corvette, but somehow it just isn't the same. A 1958 Chevrolet Impala four-door hardtop, one equipped with the 348 Tri-Power setup, might well provide sufficient roar and flash to make you happy and still offer room for the entire tribe to ride along on outings. It may well be the comfortable compromise the whole family can live with.

## Buy a Car the Whole Family Can Love

I met a man who once owned an absolutely pristine AMC Cardin Javelin. No one in his family had ever ridden in his limited edition, 100-point pride and joy, not even his wife. He attended club meets, flea markets, and car shows alone. His private time with the car became such a bone of contention that it came down to the darned Javelin or divorce papers. Reluctantly, the car was sold to a single dude in Denver.

Stylists at American Motors broke new ground in the automobile industry when they teamed up with famed European clothing designer Pierre Cardin to dress up the 1972 Javelin. The result was stunning. The boys in marketing calculated that 2,500 of the fancy-dress Javelins would sell and were astonished when 4,152 of the haute couture muscle cars hit the streets.

A man in Minnesota told me once he had never ever been allowed to climb on board and ride in his dad's 1930 Ford. As the years went by, he grew to hate the Model A and did his best to avoid seeing his dad altogether during car season. Father and son drifted apart, all over a car!

Consulting with the folks at home allows them to be part of the process from the very beginning. Discuss ways the entire family can enjoy the car. Making them part of the experience

Studebaker marked its 100th anniversary in the transportation business in 1952. A Commander State ragtop was selected to pace the Indy 500 that year but it has never achieved the price range of other pace cars.

from the initial planning stages will create anticipation and heighten the desirability of ownership. This inclusiveness guarantees maximum peace and permits maximum enjoyment. After all, the things we own should enhance and enrich the fabric of family life, not diminish and take away from it.

Relationships can be seriously damaged when a set of vintage wheels gets caught in the middle. A cherished collectible car or truck is capable of generating a surprising amount of anger, hurt, and jealousy from family members who feel left out. If Mother roars off to an MG meet every other Sunday, leaving the family behind, there will be unpleasant repercussions.

Many a family has strengthened its bonds by making the restoration and enjoyment of a collectible car a family project, one in which everyone took an active part. Those vehicles are highly prized for the special memories they have created and that car couldn't be bought, not for love nor money, not for all the black pekoe tea in the People's Republic of China.

The 1931 Cadillac V-16 Fleetwood Town Brougham weighs in at three tons and rides on a 148-inch wheelbase. It sold for $9,700 new and a basket case good only for parts would fetch the same price today.

# 2 YOU AND YOUR CAR'S SOCIAL LIFE

## Plays Well With Others?

To truly enjoy your vehicle, you need to find a comfy little niche and settle into it. You certainly won't get maximum enjoyment from your car in isolation. Cars are stars. They shine brightest in front of an audience. A great deal of the fun in owning a collector car is showing it off and letting others enjoy seeing your treasure.

People sometimes tell me they don't belong to clubs because they don't get along with the other members or dislike what they represent. If that is the case, find a club where you are comfortable.

Most clubs are nonprofit organizations dedicated to the preservation and promotion of the marque. A few clubs are privately owned and operate like any other business. Community-based clubs often work with City Hall to promote the area and local history, too.

Car shows can be lucrative for clubs and municipalities alike. An antique car show, spread over two nights and three days, can pump as much as $1.5 million into the local economy when there are 400 vehicles registered.

## Join a National Club

If you haven't already, now is the time to join a national club dedicated to the marque of vehicle that interests you. A national club is an excellent source for finding your dream wheels. Cars change hands for a myriad of reasons. The most common ones are moving, downsizing, poor health, death, divorce, or financial difficulties. Often these are "distress sales" and the cars listed are being offered at far below market value.

Ford built a car-based truck from 1957 to 1979. The Ranchero has several clubs dedicated to its preservation.

A club newsletter will not only list cars for sale, but it will also be chock full of classified advertisements for useful parts, literature, and books appropriate to your intended vehicle. You will want these in order to learn as much about your dream car as possible. Newsletters often include restoration stories, thumbnail histories, interviews with the designers and engineers, and service tips, too. You will also receive a club roster that tells who owns what and where they live.

Many national clubs are organized into state, provincial, or regional chapters that offer more frequent get-togethers, flea markets, and events. Find out about the activities of the club in your area and take in a meet.

Don't buy a 1966 Studebaker Commander only to find out afterward that the Studebaker Drivers Club in your area has been inactive for 14 years. It quickly becomes tiring to drive four hours to meet other Studebaker folks at what you initially thought would be a local gathering.

This 1947 Chrysler Town and Country Sedan is proof that not all woodies are wagons. (Photo courtesy RM Auctions, Inc.)

## Join a Specialty Club

You can join more than one club without fear of much, if any, overlapping. While you may sign up as a member of the national Oldsmobile club, if you're driving a Vista Cruiser with those neat little canted skylights, you might well decide to join one of the national station wagon clubs, too. If you let the membership director know what you've bought, the editor of the specialty club newsletter will let you know what articles have been published about your wheels, certainly pay careful attention to your model, and no doubt feature it in a future issue of the newsletter, too.

There are specialty clubs for many different kinds of vehicles. Some examples are: professional cars such as funeral cars, law enforcement vehicles, and ambulances. Other clubs focus on convertibles, micro-cars, station wagons, cars used by railroad companies, and automobiles built in a particular country like France or the UK. There are clubs for specific models, like the 1964 to 1969 Beaumont and Chevelle Club, and for orphans—vehicles no longer manufactured—and many others, too.

## Truck Clubs

Trucks and buses arrived on the roads well before automobiles. There are clubs aplenty dedicated to these honest motorized workhorses. From the pint-sized Crosley and American Bantam to the mighty Federal and gigantic GMC 18-wheelers, be sure there is a truck club to honor the marque of your choice. Two of the largest clubs for haulers are the American Historical Truck Society and the Antique Truck Club of America. Both hold national meets, provide support and technical advice to restorers, as well as publish excellent magazines.

Truck clubs generally acknowledge station wagons, too, since they are officially classified as commercial vehicles.

## Join a Local Club

You will want to become a member of a community-based club, so that you can participate in the hobby in your hometown and the surrounding area. Joining a local organization can often be another excellent source for finding parts or a set of dream wheels, as well.

Volkswagen clubs are reputed to be among the most friendly on the continent. Prices have climbed over the years but a Beetle is still an affordable vintage car. There are many clubs for fans to choose among. A 1964 VW 1500 is shown.

There are numerous clubs for the world's most posh automobile. This 1929 Rolls-Royce Phantom I Roadster, with body by Brewster, was built in the USA. (Photo courtesy RM Auctions, Inc.)

Cars from France have always had a small but staunchly loyal following. Few automobiles of the 1960s are more unusual than a 1966 Renault 10 Major. The Renault Club of North America says *bienvenue* to all who love the marque.

Your local car club often pulls together for community improvement. The organization may be raising money to build a skateboard rink for neighborhood kids, buying a CAT Scan for the hospital, or restoring a heritage building. Roll up your sleeves and flip some burgers or take on some committee work. Aside from being a good citizen, you are actually taking an active part in building a stronger, safer community. If you have kids, you are setting a good example for the next generation as you teach them civic pride. One day you might well laugh as you recall that your election to city council was an accident; it all started the night you were inspired to buy that '69 Dodge Super Bee!

**Savvy Tip**

Clubs are made up of individual people and personalities. There will always be folks who insist on bringing super-sized egos to the table. When out of control, they can dampen community spirit and destroy entire clubs. Sensible adults and good citizens check their egos at the door to enjoy the old car hobby and work together for common goals.

Without a doubt, the most sought after Japanese cars on our shores today are the Z series from Datsun. Collectors will find clubs nationally and locally. Shown here are the 1976 models.

Fans of Hupmobile should be prepared to bid up to $20,000 for a 1924 five-passenger touring car in excellent condition. Though the marque disappeared in 1940, the Hupmobile Club boasts more than 600 members worldwide.

## Join a Lifestyle Club

There are old car organizations tailored for people as well as cars. Folks are always more comfortable in familiar settings. Several religious denominations have national and regional car clubs with activities suitable to their beliefs including the Baptists, Lutherans, and Seventh-day Adventists. The Lambda Car Club serves the gay and lesbian community.

## Make Sure You Like the Club Members

A man in New York fulfilled a dream by purchasing a vintage Corvette. His motivation for doing so was based purely on the "cool" factor. He quickly discovered he disliked the attitude of the club members he encountered at meets. The quiet millionaire found the group to be cliquish, arrogant, and snobby. "Too much new money and no common sense," he told me. "They looked down on everybody else and treated new members very badly." The experiences grew negative enough that he no longer enjoyed his purchase. He finally dumped the 'Vette and purchased a 1958 Studebaker Golden Hawk with a Paxton supercharger. The Hawk satisfied the man's need for speed, and he confided to me that he was much more comfortable with the down-to-earth folks he met in the Studebaker Drivers Club. "Besides," he added, "Corvettes are common. When people see the Hawk, they flock to it and ask questions or reminisce. I love that." A woman in British Columbia shared much the same experience with me. She traded her vintage Rolls-Royce for—of all things—a Volkswagen Beetle. Her rationale was simple: "Beetle people are fun folk, not at all obsessed with image."

Before you buy a vehicle, investigate the clubs to see if you are comfortable with the people in the club. You won't enjoy your car nearly as much if you don't like the folks you will see regularly at shows and swap meets!

## Make New Friends

If your national car club is holding its annual meet in some faraway, exotic part of the continent you've always wanted to visit, you now have the perfect excuse for planning a once in a lifetime holiday around the event. You will get to know your car and your family. You will see new places and make new friends. There are few quality moments in life as precious as those spent with loved ones and a favorite collectible car.

Fords imported from Britain are always of interest and the North American English & European Ford Registry offers support and a newsletter. Withdrawn from the US at the end of 1969, British Fords continued to be popular in Canada until the rise of the Pound Sterling drove them out of the market at the end of 1973. A 1971 Ford Cortina GT is seen here.

The National Woodie Club preserves and promotes wooden-bodied vehicles, a.k.a. "woodies." Seen here is the very rare 1950 Monarch wagon, built by the Ford Motor Company of Canada, Limited. Only three examples are known to be in existence today.

Don't be the least bit surprised as you tool along in your collector car by strangers who approach you on the road and greet you like long lost kin. This happens often, and they are unforgettable experiences. In the backwoods of the Badger State, I parked my 1969 AMC Ambassador at a fast food joint. An elderly couple waved their double burgers in the air and offered an invitation to come eat with them. Of course we had an instant topic of conversation: we talked about cars. The gentleman had worked for Nash-Kelvinator and American Motors down in Kenosha years ago.

They graciously invited me home with them to show me their entire collection of very cool collector cars. They had a Mitchell, a Kissel, and a host of Nash and Rambler cars too, all manufactured in Wisconsin. Drooling over all that chrome made us hungry and that led to a fine dinner of steaks smothered in four Wisconsin cheeses, mashed potatoes, and sauerkraut. A truly unforgettable blackberry pie appeared, with coffee, for dessert. I thanked them for the wonderful time, gave them an autographed copy of my history of American Motors, and bid my hosts goodbye with handshakes and hugs. I drove away, loaded down to the axles with goodies, including a half-gallon jug of homemade maple syrup. We exchanged Christmas cards for years.

Those good folks have gone to their rest, but our chance encounter still warms my heart. A friendship formed and cemented over a love of old cars transcending state lines, national borders, language barriers, and any other obstacle one might care to toss into the mix. Sparked by a common interest, this kind of friendship is of the most meaningful quality, truly a fitting symbol of life in today's Global Village.

# 3 REPAIRS, MAINTENANCE, AND COST

## Calculate Costs

No matter how well restored your vintage vehicle is, it will always require regular maintenance. That magnificent, head-turning 1959 Oldsmobile will also need special care simply because it is an older set of wheels. If you hanker after a brand of car no longer manufactured like a 1948 Hudson, when it does come time for maintenance and repairs, prices for parts will be more expensive. For the uninitiated, 6-volt batteries, magnetos, and authentic period rayon tires all cost more than you might expect.

On the other hand, some parts are not expensive at all, depending on the vehicle's longevity in the marketplace. Many a joke has been made about being able to build a Ford Model T from scratch with new parts ordered from the J.C. Whitney catalog. Any time I needed engine parts for my 1969 AMC Ambassador, they were readily available, right off the shelf at NAPA and Canadian Tire because the trusty AMC sixes and V-8 engines were still being used in Jeeps more than two decades later. It is wise to know what parts interchange.

Sometimes a former dealer will still have parts on hand. I once needed some repair work done to the Ambassador while in Philadelphia. The police kindly directed me to the Chrysler-Jeep dealer who had been a longtime AMC and Rambler dealer before Chrysler bought American Motors in 1987. The dealer principal himself came flying out the door when he spotted the Ambassador and hollered, "Get that car out of here! We're not fixing any Ramblers!"

Ford's 1914 Model T Touring Car, with its planetary transmission is simple to operate and fun to drive.

On the other hand, I was at a swap meet in Baltimore where I found mirrors for my 1966 Rambler convertible. The car had been given to Miss Canada. I wanted to drive home with the mirrors in place. The local Chevrolet dealer used to handle Ramblers. The car went right into the service area, and the dealer hovered while the mechanic bolted them on, all the while regaling me with stories about the years when he and his dad sold Ramblers. He didn't even charge me for the installation. All he wanted was to drive the sassy Rambler for a couple of miles and have his picture taken with it.

Don't be afraid to purchase used parts, but do make note of this: when replacing a worn- out part with a used one, a careful inspection is in order. Because your oil pump needs replacing, it is highly probable that the used oil pump you purchase may not be in tip-top condition, either.

Miss Canada's 1966 Rambler American is owned by Dominic Sauve of Montreal. Rambler purists will note the Canada-only wheel covers.

## Using Wrong Parts Costs Money

My 1963 Studebaker Lark Daytona developed power steering problems. The car would simply veer off the road to the right, even though my hands were firmly on the wheel. It was a completely unnerving experience. I had the power steering unit completely rebuilt, but the problem persisted. A second rebuild didn't solve the problem, either. I was afraid to drive the Lark after leaving the road and coming to a rather embarrassing stop in a pasture. The herd of Holsteins was amused at the unexpected company, but I certainly wasn't!

I talked about the steering failure to everyone I could think of, and one day a friend told me he knew an elderly man who had been a Studebaker mechanic at a local dealership for many years. The gentleman had gotten so good at troubleshooting he had been hired by the head office to fly around North America and solve quirky problems. Now in his 80s, and not in the best of health, the gentleman graciously agreed to take on the case of the mysterious steering failure. He lived less than an hour away, and I was surprised I had never heard of him. Painstakingly thorough, it took him nearly a year to find the source of the problem. A replacement washer, located at the base of the unit was a few millimeters too thick, causing the power steering unit to fail. I was highly pleased that the problem was finally solved, even though my wallet was a good $3,000 lighter by the end of the ordeal.

Surprisingly low in price today, the 1967 AMC Ambassador offers a sumptuous ride.

## Substitute Parts When it Makes Sense

I owned a 1967 Ambassador sedan that made its living as a movie car. When it wasn't sparkling in front of the cameras, I drove it for the sheer pleasure and comfort of its ride. I certainly wasn't overly concerned about originality and authenticity, especially where it could not be readily seen. When the exhaust system needed replacing, my mechanic simply took one from a scrapped Volkswagen that fit perfectly. The cost came to $24 for the transplant, and no one was any the wiser.

## Make Sure Parts and Service Are Available

No matter how much you love your Duesenberg, Viking, or your Cartercar, you can't run down to the local dealer for parts. Those dealerships are long gone. A car can be laid up for months while you attempt to locate a part. It is hard to enjoy a vehicle that doesn't run. A car that is off the road for a long period of time can sour your experience as a collector. If you are desirous of owning a long-vanished marque, be prepared to pay big bucks and stockpile parts when you find them. If the car was not common when it was new, parts for it will be even more difficult to source today. Sometimes the part no longer exists, and one will have to be machined for you.

Some cars are too exotic to be worked on easily. Mechanics in your area might not know how to restore or even repair your car. A judge in rural Indiana owned a vintage Rolls-Royce. It was his daily driver, but His Honor had great difficulty in finding parts for it and an even worse time finding someone who could keep it on the road. Finally, he paid a local mechanic to go to Chicago and take a Rolls-Royce course in order to have help at the ready, should problems develop. The solution was unique and worked out fine for both the judge and the mechanic.

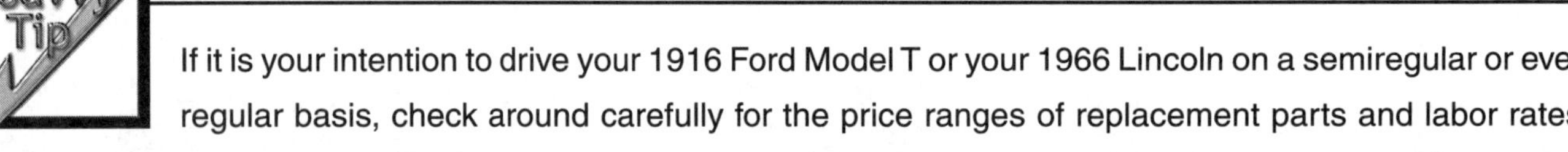


If it is your intention to drive your 1916 Ford Model T or your 1966 Lincoln on a semiregular or even regular basis, check around carefully for the price ranges of replacement parts and labor rates, too. If parts for your wheels are difficult to locate and costly, and labor rates will bankrupt you, consider another vehicle.

## Know Your Garage

There are garages that will offer to repair your vehicle, but they may not be reputable. It is imperative that you shop around. Find out if other collectible car owners have used their services and come away satisfied. Take a tour of the facilities. If you see lots of older cars being worked on, that's a good thing. Another encouraging sign of an understanding garage is letters of thanks from different car clubs or happy owners, framed and hanging on the walls of the waiting room.

A friend in Florida took his cherished 1956 Hudson Metropolitan to a shop for a ground up restoration. Unfortunately, the only mechanic who knew how to work on it quit. The Met got shoved unceremoniously into the far corner of the shop to gather dust. When the exasperated owner finally realized that no one was ever going to work on his Met, he brought a tow truck to the shop with the intention of having it hauled away. To his astonishment the garage was empty; his beloved Met had disappeared. Despite the police department's best efforts to locate it, the shop's new location was never found. The search ended at a post office box address. More than three years later, the Met was recovered. Its burnt-out remains were discovered deep in a pine forest by a Boy Scout troop.

Parts are fairly easy to source for this luxurious 1966 Lincoln Continental.

## Know Where to Get Service on the Road

I quickly learned that it was essential to keep a list of garages, sources, and other owners at my fingertips. The air-conditioning quit on my car in August in South Carolina. By the time I arrived in Maryland, I was as sick as a dog from the heat, registering in excess of 130 degrees Fahrenheit inside the cabin. I called an old car buddy in Pennsylvania and managed to get to the Keystone State. He kindly arranged a motel in Bethlehem and when I felt better, took the ailing Ambassador and me to a garage where understanding mechanics were familiar with older cars.

Once we determined what parts were needed, my buddy and I made a trek to Rambler Mountain—no, I am not making this up—to visit a man who had acres and acres of Ramblers and AMC passenger cars scattered all over his Appalachian property. With the help of a trusty screwdriver, the parts I needed were removed from rusty hulks. That set me back $11. The labor came to $102. Once the bill was settled, I was right back on the road with a properly functioning air-conditioning unit.

Be extremely wary of places that don't have a clue as to what they're working on. When my Ambassador required roadside assistance once in New York, the tow truck driver was not

As pretty as this 1926 Oakland is, GM no longer stocks parts for it. The marque went to old car heaven in 1931.

pleased with my choice of garages. "Why don't you bring it to our place?" he asked. "We have plenty of experience working on these old Buicks." If he didn't know the difference between an American Motors car and a GM product, I certainly didn't want him fumbling around under the hood of my precious baby! I firmly declined the offer and insisted the Ambassador be towed to the repair shop initially specified. The mechanics there specialized in AMC, Studebaker-Packard, and 1950s Chrysler products. So loyal were Dick and Raymond Tucker to old Detroit iron, a big sign out front of the garage warned, "Jap Scrap Not Welcome!" After hearing a description of the problem, the mechanic knew where to look. An hour and $25 later, the problem was solved, and I was back on the interstate.

**Savvy Tip**

Keep a list of garages, sources for parts, and a list of owners who have a vehicle similar to yours in the glove box of your collectible car. Once you join a car club, you will receive a parts and source guide generated by club members. These are passed along to all members periodically in printed form. The guide will prove to be invaluable when traveling.

No, this is not a Vauxhall. This 1951 Ford Vedette rides a 100-inch wheelbase. Originally planned for the post-war North American market, management nixed its introduction at the last minute and sent the baby Mercury look-alike to France.

## Shop Repair and Parts Manuals

Do track down and buy the shop repair manual. Two of the biggest and best sources in the world are Walter Miller and Ken McGee. These boys also have sales brochures, something every wise owner of a collectible car will want to have on hand. Where manuals and brochures are no longer readily available, some clubs have reprinted them. For most post-war vehicles, you will find originals at swap meets. These books were used in the garage to repair vehicles, so expect them to have some well-worn, grease-stained pages. Like parts, finding manuals and printed material is always luck of the draw. I turned down a shop manual in Tampa because it carried a $300 price but, by chance, found one in much better shape a month later for $70 at a swap meet in Toronto.

More than once I have had to use the emergency services of a modern garage where mechanics thought that Studebaker was a Chrysler product or Vauxhall was a French Ford. Despite their ignorance, the mechanics could all read the service manual I had in the car and that simplified the situation greatly.

Parts manuals are also important. Each part is illustrated and listed by number so that it can be referred to when ordering. These manuals also show detailed exploded diagrams that show how each part fits with the next to make a complete subassembly.

Shop repair manuals and parts manuals are essential. They can be books, but they are often loose-leaf sheets in a large binder. In many cases they cover multiple years. If that is the case with yours, consider preserving the pages by slipping them into plastic page protectors.

## Parts Exchange Books

Become acquainted with the various parts exchange books. These are long lists that spell out what part will interchange in various automobiles or trucks. I could have spent a small fortune sourcing original shocks for the Ambassador wagon, but the Monroe shock absorber parts exchange book showed that Cadillac Eldorado shocks up to 1979 fit the front of my wagon while rear shocks were the same as those used on Ford Econoline vans right through the 1980s. Most garages and large auto parts stores have parts exchange books. Exchanges aren't limited

Sisters under the skin, the 1957 Packard shared its mechanicals with the Studebaker line. Only 869 of the posh Clipper Country Sedans left the factory during the model year.

to cars and trucks, either. When my 1963 Studebaker Standard needed roller bearings for the front wheels, my wise and highly experienced mechanic sent me to the John Deere dealership for a set that fit perfectly.

## Insurance

Consider who will drive the vehicle. Insurance premiums will soar through the stratosphere if a teen or inexperienced driver gets behind the wheel. If you decide to pull a vintage trailer behind your vehicle, insurance rates will go up appreciably, too. Your broker should be able to help you, but if not, there are companies that cater to the collector car crowd, offering special rates and discounts. Among the big insurance underwriters in the United States are Aon and Hagerty. In Canada, it is Silver Wheels.

The Packard Motor Car Company purchased the Studebaker Corporation in 1954. The two brands shared body shells and mechanical components in 1957 and 1958. The President Classic was the most popular Studebaker in 1957; 6,063 units were built.

## Storage

Don't even think of buying a collectible car until you have lined up proper parking and storage for it! Where will you keep your purchase when it's not on the road? Is there room for it in the family garage? Your precious vehicle deserves a special place.

A gentleman in Alabama went to great lengths and expense to buy the automobile in which he was born. It needed some work but was in pretty good shape. Always intending to get around to it, he left the car outside, exposed to the elements. The years passed, and by the time he was ready to lavish some attention on it, the once beautiful Ford had disintegrated to the point of no longer being restorable.

The Cartercar had no gears; it used a friction transmission. General Motors' management pulled the plug on the brand in 1915. A 1909 Model H Touring car is seen here. (Photo courtesy RM Auctions, Inc.)

If you do not have on-site parking, you will have to drive to a space that you rent or own. The logistics of packing a picnic into the daily sedan then driving a half hour only to reload everything into that 1966 Thunderbird before hitting the road quickly loses its appeal. You will use the car less and less until finally it sits, gathering dust, unloved and unused.

Storage must be dry in order to prevent rust, mildew, and mold. It must also be free of rodents. You don't want to discover that mice have made nests out of your backseats or squirrels gnawed through your hoses during the winter months. If the space isn't heated, well lit, and well ventilated, you certainly won't enjoy tinkering with your car during the cold months.

You may opt to build a dream garage. Some of my favorites are those where owners have carpeted their garages and decorated one end with period living rooms. It is heavenly to lean back on the *I Love Lucy* vintage sectional sofa in a re-creation of Lucy and Ricky Ricardo's New York City apartment while gazing at the lovingly restored 1955 Pontiac.

### Meet Dean Kruse — Kruse International

Dean Kruse was born in 1941 on a card table in a farmhouse near Auburn, Indiana. The family milked 63 head of dairy cows, and young Dean vowed early on that whatever he did in life it wouldn't be dairy farming! Auctions were always part of his life; his first auction memory is of going to events with his grandfather, Lester E. Boger, an auction clerk. Dean's dad was not just a farmer; Russell Kruse was also an auctioneer. His dad started taking him along to auctions when he was 11. Dean's first job in the business was to hold up the item being sold. Displaying a pair of bolt cutters while his dad auctioned them off, Dean followed his dad's instructions and began looking for the next item to hold up for the crowd to keep the auction's momentum flowing.

Dean's first taste at the podium was when he was 14. His dad was selling out a grocery store and needed to go to the bathroom. "Son," he said, "sell some items while I take a break." Dean jumped right up there on the podium, selling jams and jellies by the jar. Strawberry jelly started at 20 cents. He sold them off and moved to the raspberry and apricot varieties. By now, his dad was in the back of the room, watching the budding auctioneer. When Dean got to the currant jelly, he started it at 10 cents instead of 20 cents. The hammer went down on the currant jelly at 13 cents a bottle. When his dad asked him why he lowered the price, Dean replied, "Because I don't like currant jelly, and it ought to sell for less." Russell understood his son's sense of values and told him he was right to lower the price. That day Russell Kruse knew he had a genuine auctioneer offspring.

Growing up in Dekalb County, Dean attended Leo High School. His dad's auction business was getting bigger all the time, and Russell turned to Dean for help. Dean liked the idea of

*Young Dean perfecting his craft*

being a partner. He attended Reppert's Auction School in Decatur, Indiana, between his junior and senior year in high school. It was there that the teen learned the art of auctioneering. Dean recalls, "It was the oldest auction school in the nation and, eventually, I bought it."

With a craft already under his belt, the principal told Dean he could miss school for business reasons and still graduate as long as he kept his grades up. He missed more than 40 school days that final year, but his grades were fine, and he marched down the aisle as part of the Class of 1958.

*Mr. Kruse with President George W. Bush and First Lady Laura Bush*

Dean asked folks of prominence and influence in and around Auburn if he should go to college or go into business with his dad. To a man, they all advised him to get an education first. Dean realized that not a one of them had followed the advice so freely given to him. He compromised by studying law through the LaSalle University Extension program from Chicago.

The business boomed in the late 1950s and early 1960s. There were lots of sales, real estate, and farm auctions. Dean remembers that in February of 1959 the company conducted 45 auctions in 30 days! Dean, like every auctioneer, has a favorite warm-up tongue twister. His is: "Theopholis thistle the famous thistle sifter in sifting 3,000 unsifted thistles thrust a thistle through the thick of his thumb."

He married childhood sweetheart Carol Yoder in 1960. Time and the extreme demands of running a nationwide auction business caused them to drift apart, and they divorced amicably in 1994. Their two sons, Mitchell and Stuart, joined their dad in the auction business. Dean remembers that when Mitchell was six, he helped out by carrying tickets up to the clerk at the office. One rainy day Mitchell got stuck in the mud and couldn't move. Two big burly gents came along and lifted him up by his arms. The mud was so deep and so thick that Mitchell's boots stayed stuck in the gumbo.

While in high school, Dean was chosen by the local American Legion to attend Boys' State Convention, a hands-on exercise in civics. There are mock committees, a county chairman, a state chairman, cabinet ministers, a lieutenant governor, and a governor. Dean worked his way up to state auditor and was the only one on his team's ticket who won in the mock election. It was more than a lesson for Dean.

When he was 21, Dean ran for the office of Dekalb County chairman. Because of the vicious attacks the two better-known candidates made on each other, Dean squeaked through and won the three-way race by two votes. It was a start in politics. At 25, he filed for state senator and won the election on the Republican ticket. He was the Indiana legislature's liaison to the White House during the Nixon administration.

Dean quit politics to return to the business. He noted that there were no consignment sales of collector cars in the United States. Now, Forke Brothers in Lincoln, Nebraska, had started an annual heavy equipment sale, and Dean mused over the idea of doing the same thing with antique cars. At about the same time, the Auburn Chamber of Commerce came to Russell, looking for a way to support their involvement with the annual Auburn Cord Duesenberg Festival without losing the $5,000 a year they had sustained in past years. They wanted Russell to auction off items donated by the merchants. Russell shared with them Dean's idea of selling vintage cars on consignment.

They gave it a shot in 1971. Leo Gephart, a classic car advisor, was brought in to authenticate the cars being sold. Dean was hurrying home from working a Yoder and Fry heavy equipment event in West Virginia. The roads were jammed with traffic, no matter which route he tried. At first he thought it was a long train that was holding up the works, and suddenly it dawned on him that these cars were on their way to the auction house.

That first collector car auction was an astonishing success. Men had been stationed at the entry to collect a one dollar a head fee. They racked up $7,800 before the crowd knocked down the steel ropes. An estimated 30,000 people attended, and 63 cars crossed the block. If the Kruse clan was surprised, the merchants were flabbergasted. Visitors had literally cleaned out all the grocery stores. The event got the attention of CBS, NBC, and ABC, all of which sent crews to cover the event and ran it as a national news story. The second sale was with Tom Barrett in Arizona, and the rest is history.

Kruse International sold the William F. Harris collection of classic and vintage cars for $41.5 million in 1987 and 1988. The company sells more than cars; it sold Marina Towers in Chicago for $22.75 million. It sold Lindsey Downs, a horse racetrack in Louisiana, and several automobile racetracks. Dean chuckles when he says he has auctioned off three whole towns! Jones, Michigan; Rockerville, South Dakota; and a small town in the Ozarks have all had the Kruse hammer fall on them.

Falling in love, he married Kristin McGrade in 1999. She was an All-American basketball star at Indiana University. They wanted a family but were told it would take two years to adopt.

At the Indianapolis 500, Dean's friend Burl Keener had his grandson on his lap. Dean was surprised; he knew that Burl's daughter couldn't have children. He learned that the child had been adopted through an organization called Hand in Hand. It specialized in matching up American parents with Russian orphans. A picture of an adorable baby from Hand in Hand caught the couple's attention, and they made preparations for the adoption.

*Mr. Kruse at an auction*

A couple of weeks later, just before Christmas, Dean flew on his private Challenger to St. Petersburg, Russia. The plane landed at 4 a.m. to clear Customs and to take on a Russian crew. He had $15,000 cash in new $100 bills as required for the transaction. He took along $60,000 just in case anything went wrong with the jet. He stashed the cash in an Orvis fishing jacket with all the pockets and threw a sports coat over it. Realizing he needed protection, he had called his friend Dennis Hastert who happened to be the Speaker of the House in Washington, D.C. Dennis had recommended a bodyguard who turned out to be a former KGB agent, and Dean had hired him. While airport security in St. Petersburg counted his $60,000, the Russian pilot had a screaming match with the former KGB agent because he was toting a gun on the plane.

They arrived in Saratov, a city of 2.5 million people in the south of Russia. Dean was struck by the abject poverty and squalid living conditions of the Russian people. The plane landed on the rough tarmac filled with enormous potholes. Military vehicles stopped the plane half a mile from the terminal and wouldn't let it any closer. Dean asked the officers to allow the plane to approach the terminal so they could unload the toys he had brought for the orphans. He was told "no" in Russian. Spotting an old truck from the 1940s, it was agreed he could use that to load and transport the toys. The general, a little miffed, told Dean the children didn't need toys; they needed medicine. Dean didn't forget. When he returned, he brought a planeload of medicine, a gift from Wal-Mart.

The general sent a van for Dean and his guard, the former KGB agent. The two spent 15 minutes at Customs doing absolutely nothing but watching an officer examine their passports. Finally they were stamped, and the people from the orphanage arrived to pick them up. The army officers softened a bit and loaded the toys on the truck for them.

Dean handed out American two-dollar bills to the men as a gesture of good will, but the general said it was against regulations to accept foreign money. Thinking fast, Dean explained that while they were legal tender in the United States, two-dollar bills are rarely seen by the public and given only as good luck charms, not ever to be spent. The Russians accepted. Happy to be cleared, Dean impulsively gave the general, who looked like Kruschev, a big old bear hug, and he got one back! The general became human. He allowed the plane to taxi up to the terminal and had guards watch it until they returned.

Knowing that Russian hotels can be tough places, Dean asked for the best suite in the hotel. A three-room suite cost $68 a night, but he couldn't have it because it was reserved for the local political leader, if he came to town. He was shown to another room that was like stepping back into the 1920s.

The orphanage liaisons took Dean to the wrong orphanage four times. They were sad places and reminded him of miniature prison camps. At the first one, a 10-year-old answered the door and led them up to the matron. The boy's expression haunted Dean; he couldn't shake the look for weeks. At the fifth orphanage, Dean completed the transaction and went home. He brooded about the first boy, and after discussing it with Kristin, he decided to return to Russia and adopt him, too.

*Mr. Kruse with Jay Leno*

Today, that little boy is sure God helped him find Dean and Kristin. He told his adopted parents that one day when he was supposed to be at school he was playing outside and fell into the garbage dump. He found a picture of Jesus and took it back to the orphanage. He cleaned it up, mounted it, and put it on the wall. He had been reading the printed prayer under the Savior's face the day he met Dean. The boys, now ages seven and 15, have adjusted to the American way of life and are thrilled to be part of a real family. They intend to be auctioneers when they grow up, too.

As of 2006, Dean has conducted more than 8,000 auctions, and he also marks his 50th year in the business. The Auburn show is hitting near the $100 million mark annually, and more than 150,000 attend this event, one of the largest private property sales in the world. Dean has no plans to retire. When his Maker calls him, he will no doubt have a microphone in his hand.

# 4 WHEN A CAR IS AN INVESTMENT

A car that is being purchased for investment purposes will almost always be one that sold with a fairly hefty price tag when it was new. Any of the traditional Classics fit that bill, so do luxury makes after 1948 such as Cadillac and Lincoln. Many of the cars that fall into this category will be heavily optioned with extra-cost equipment. These cars will be matching numbers, 100-point show cars, or as close to that magic number as possible. They will come with papers, including a build sheet and an owner history, available from the Department or Ministry of Motor Vehicles. If previous owners were meticulous, your vehicle will come with complete repair records to boot.

Savvy Tip

Most states and provinces have registration records on vehicles that reach back at least to the early 1970s, some even further. For a fee, you can trace ownership of your car, at least as far as the government has maintained records.

## Gold from Rust

Brian Carlson is an auction reporter for *Old Cars*. He attended a farm auction in Verenderye, North Dakota. One of the lots up for sale was a 1931 Nash 890 four-door sedan. "Well, it was the residue of a Nash, anyway," Brian recalls with a chuckle. "It had been dragged out of a shed three years earlier and once exposed to the elements, the wooden frame gave way and the body collapsed on itself. The interior was gone, the body had caved in." Now, clearly this is no 100-point show car, but the 1931 Nash was a luxurious vehicle, and the 890 series has been granted the coveted Classic status by the Classic Car Club of America (CCCA). The headlights, grille, and grille guards on this one were still in very good shape. The auctioneer got the bid to $100 for the rusty remains, but the hammer went down for Brian at $300. He now owned what had once been a magnificent Nash. He resold the battered hulk to an avid collector who was extremely keen to be in possession of the rare parts that remained.

### Proof of Ownership

This document shows legal proof of ownership and gives a history of the vehicle. In the United States, it is called the title. At auctions, the title is sometimes "In Transit" and not available for viewing. Be wary of a vehicle with a title you cannot see. It may be on hand tomorrow, may take six months to arrive, or it may not ever come at all.

A 1965 Corvette is a good investment.

**Savvy Tip**

The vehicle title system is not used in Canada. The provincial and territorial Ministries of Transport have simplified ownership by recognizing the registration as legal proof of ownership. Once the old owner signs off that portion of the paper, the vehicle belongs to you.

---

## Matching Numbers

Matching numbers ensure that the engine, chassis, and body are original. The engine's serial number is stamped on it, usually on the block. There will be a chassis number somewhere on the frame and a body number on the body as well. On older vehicles, these three numbers will all be recorded on a metal build tag, usually located on the inner doorsill or riveted to the glove box. If the numbers stamped on that tag don't match the numbers on the engine, frame, and body, the value of the vehicle is considerably reduced. This isn't terribly important if the car under consideration is being purchased strictly for your driving pleasure. It becomes more of an issue if you are collecting for the purpose of watching an investment rise in value. Corvette owners like to joke that all 5,000 of the 3,754 Corvettes built in 1965 equipped with the 435-cubic-inch engine have been accounted for!

Those matching numbers on the build tag include original paint codes, too. A man from Pennsylvania told me he was more than a little uncomfortable with the original Shell Pink over Iridescent Metallic Grey paint job that adorned his 1955 DeSoto. He was much happier to drive around in a DeSoto finished in Coronado Green over Black, a dramatic two-tone color combination that appeared late in the model year. The value of the man's DeSoto dropped dramatically the minute the paint scheme no longer matched the paint code stamped on the manufacturer's build tag.

This 1934 Packard Twelve Convertible Victoria with coachwork by Dietrich is not just elegant, it is a symbol of all that is refined. Classic cars like this can easily top $1 million at auctions. (Photo courtesy RM Auctions)

## Build Sheets

A build sheet is the physical piece of paper that accompanied your vehicle down the lines in the factory while it was being assembled. This paper shows all the components and options ordered and built into the car, the date of manufacture of the body and engine, the date of completion, and the date of shipment to the initial distributor or dealer. In many cars, workers at the end of the line stuffed the build sheet up into the springs under the rear seat or behind the instrument panel once everything was checked off and the car was complete.

A Milestone Car like this 1957 Chevrolet Bel Air convertible can bring as much as $50,000 at an auction. (Photo courtesy RM Auctions)

Lucky owners sometimes find the build sheet intact, often still hiding in the back seat springs or behind the dash. Folks not so fortunate can generally acquire a build sheet from the manufacturer, if the company is still in existence. To date, Ford does not charge for this service. Others, like GM Canada's Heritage Services, charge a modest fee. In the case of vehicles no longer built, clubs may have them, or they may be available through private companies. Studebaker Autoparts Sales Corporation (SASCO) has many of the build sheets for Studebaker cars and trucks.

The late Dale Earnhardt owned this 1969 Chevrolet Camaro SS. He had it prepared in his professional race shop for his own personal use. (Photo courtesy of RM Auctions)

## Authentication Papers

If Marilyn Monroe, Pope John XXIII, or Wayne Gretzky once owned the car you want to buy, a notarized statement will attest to that fact. George Washington didn't sleep in half the beds one would have you believe, and Elvis didn't own every pink Cadillac convertible that's up for sale, either. If you are being told that your vehicle is a 100-point Antique Car Club of America (ACCA) winner, you will want to see the accompanying certificate and paperwork that testifies to the prizes awarded. Restoration should be documented with images and papers. Properly documented papers authenticate a claim. These are all part of your vehicle's pedigree and attest to its heritage and its value.

The late Pope John-Paul II owned this modest Ford Escort. It crossed the block at a Kruse auction.

## Storage

To showcase its beauty and safeguard its value, there is not a snowball's chance in a microwave oven that your investment car will be the one you drive down to the A&W on Tuesday nights for a root beer float. That vehicle will spend the vast majority of its time cocooned in a climate-controlled home of its own and be transported in a climate-controlled trailer to important shows and posh Concours d'Elegances for high-stakes judging.

Like a fine sable coat or diamonds, an investment vehicle requires special storage. Be prepared to spend money for a heated and air-conditioned garage, a truck for hauling, and an enclosed trailer, if your car is intended as a hedge against the future. Oh, you will need tuxedos and evening gowns, too; a Concours d'Elegance is a true, star-studded gala, drawing a virtual Who's Who of society. You will rub shoulders with Hollywood stars, captains of industry, top auto executives, and VIPs, all because you share a common passion for fine, older cars.

## Value

Like any other commodity, the values for vintage cars tend to run in cycles. It has been noted by analysts that desirability for the purchase of a set of antique wheels traditionally runs counter to stock market activity. Forecasters chart trends for collectible cars using sales data and leading economic indicators to chart probable projections. For a good decade and more, bullet-nosed Studebakers were hot; prices rose and the South Bend beauty fetched a pretty penny. Now, the price has peaked, that is to say, their desirability has cooled off considerably. Every car has its day in the sun. My parents turned down $40,000 for their 1930 Ford Model A in the late 1980s, but they are not nearly that expensive, today. If you are buying a set of wheels as an investment, choose carefully.

Prices for Ford's Model A peaked in the $40,000 range a decade ago. Today they cost much less. A 1930 Deluxe Roadster is shown.

This top-of-the-line 1958 Studebaker President hardtop coupe is expected to run as high as $14,700 at an auction while a 1958 Chevrolet Impala hardtop can hit the $28,000 mark.

If your car has unusual packages or options, check the value guide references to see how much one should add or take away from the estimated price. A 1979 Oldsmobile loses 10 percent if it is equipped with the V-6 or diesel engine. Add 10 percent to the price of a 1963 Mercury Monterey if it wears Custom trim. Add 30 percent onto that same Monterey if it has a 406 cid engine and push that price up by 60 percent if its workers stuffed a 427-cid engine under the hood.

Desirability grew and prices rose for the previously overlooked 1962 Rambler American convertible when it was paired off with a space alien family on the TV sitcom, *3rd Rock from the Sun.*

## Never Speculate

Automotive magazines frequently publish retrospective articles about particular models that their editors and contributors believe are on the verge of becoming future collectibles. That's nice of them, but they aren't the ones buying. You are thinking of buying, and you can't afford to speculate. Far too many folks snap up cars willy-nilly, expecting them to soar in value almost over night because they read it in a magazine.

A 1955 Chevrolet Bel Air in excellent shape will bring anywhere from $18,000 to $25,000 on sale day. (Photo courtesy RM Auctions)

A woman in Indiana recently showed me her gorgeous 1975 Buick Le Sabre Custom convertible. With only 17 miles on the odometer, the tri-shield ragtop still smelled new inside. She ordered it from the manufacturer on spec, figuring since it was the last convertible to be built, it would rise quickly in value. Buick paced the Indianapolis 500 that year, and among the 40 cars decked out for official use, a small number of Le Sabre convertibles were included. Surprisingly, the big Buick soft top has not risen greatly in value.

Paul Lehman of Pottsville, Pennsylvania, bought a 1987 Renault Alliance convertible because he had read it was about to shoot up in price. The only thing that rose was his blood pressure while waiting impatiently for big bucks that never did appear. Fortunately, he enjoys driving the saucy Cabriolet with the Gallic accent, and when he does sell it, he will not only make his money back, he can add many new pleasurable motoring memories to an already extensive bank.

Designer Brooks Stevens revamped the 1962 Studebaker lineup. He gave it a deliberate Mercedes-Benz look. Studebaker was sole distributor of M-B cars in North America at the time.

I met a young couple in Massachusetts who initially intended to invest money in their future by purchasing a vintage Mercedes-Benz. The more they studied Mercedes, the more displeased they became at what they felt were the inflated prices. During their research, they discovered that a company by the name of Studebaker owned the North American distributorship rights for M-B from 1956 to 1966. That caused them to investigate Studebaker, a marque they were not familiar with, at all. Eventually they settled on the purchase of a 1962 Studebaker Lark, largely because it bore more than a passing resemblance to Mercedes cars of the era. The model they chose had the added distinction of being the official Pace Car at that year's Indianapolis 500. The Lark was a happy compromise, and as they became skilled in the art of buying and selling collectible Studebakers, they made good money, too.

## Limited Editions and Anniversary Editions

Another common trap first-time buyers must avoid is speculation on special anniversary editions of cars or ones that were supposedly built in limited numbers. Folks who snapped up Silver Anniversary Corvettes in 1978 in hopes of a quick buck are just now beginning to get their money's worth. That special model is now worth 10 percent more than ordinary Corvettes built that year. If it carries the Indianapolis 500 Pace Car markings, it is now worth 30 percent above the average price.

By 1969 there was a California GS, a GS 350, and a GS 400 in the Buick stable, all riding on the Skylark chassis. A GS 400 hardtop is shown.

A genuine 1967 or 1968 Buick Skylark GS California is a rare bird, but factory officials did not keep track of the final tally. So many ordinary Skylarks have been "made over" into GS California models that the chances of owning the Real McCoy are about as probable as Frosty the Snowman getting through July in Georgia.

Gary Bennett is the senior automotive specialist at Barrett-Jackson. He does the verification and research on cars presented by potential sellers. His job is to make sure the car is what the seller says it is. "Due diligence is required to avoid fraud," he says and points out that there are

It is relatively easy to turn any modest 1964 Pontiac LeMans into a GTO since the company offered the GTO package in any of its LeMans models. This is one of the most often cloned cars on the auction block today.

attempts to defraud buyers. Most of these attempts are unwitting, however. Recently someone wanted to place a Buick Skylark GS in the Barrett-Jackson event. Gary discovered that it was an ordinary Buick Skylark being passed off as the highly desirable GS model. The seller had no idea. He had purchased the car from a celebrity who sold it as a GS. Gary's due diligence corrected the situation. The Skylark was accepted for sale once it was properly reidentified as a clone. Gary says that as many as 50 vehicles a year presented for sale are misidentified, and Barrett-Jackson's team sets them right.

The 1967 Buick Skylark California GS was first introduced on the West Coast. This lean, mean muscle car was then offered throughout the United States in 1968 and was specially trimmed with deluxe chrome, Kelsey-Hayes wheels, a vinyl top, and unique side moldings. The rear fender skirts seen on other Skylarks were omitted on the California GS. It had its own steering wheel and carried California script on the grille, roof panels, and the rear fenders along with a GS emblem on the rear deck lid. Most importantly, the mighty 340-cid mill was stuffed under its hood, giving it the capacity to scoot from 0 to 60 miles per hour in 6.6 seconds with a standard tranny and 6.9 seconds with the automatic shifter. Buick did not record how many of the specially trimmed two-door coupes were ever built, so the final count will always remain a mystery.

## Clones

When a base model of a particular vehicle or one of lesser interest is turned into a better, more desirable model with upgrades and badging, it is called a clone. One of the first cars to be cloned or passed off as something it wasn't was the 1964 Pontiac Lemans GTO. Now, a real GTO is worth significantly more than an ordinary LeMans that has been dressed up. Another vehicle that is often cloned is the Plymouth Barracuda AAR with the 426 Hemi. Many 1959 Cadillac Coupe de Villes got their tops chopped and presto! They became convertibles at a body shop. Cloning has become so common that auction houses now introduce them as such, and the once-phony car has gained a legitimate place in the hobby as a desirable purchase.

A 1965 Pontiac GTO will fetch between $20,000 and $40,000 on the block. This one is not a clone; it's the real McCoy.

**Savvy Tip**

A clone car becomes a fraud car if the owner attempts to pass the vehicle off as an original example of the make. If you want an original and want to be certain, do your homework diligently or consider paying an expert to come along and authenticate the specimen so you don't buy an imitation accidentally.

Another frequently cloned vehicle is the 1970 Plymouth Barracuda. Many folks like to upgrade it to the AAR version.

## Cars as Stars

There's no accounting for what will be hot down the road. Sometimes a particular car is featured in a movie or a television series, and prices rise sharply as a result of media exposure. The *Starsky and Hutch* Torino is a good example of a star car. Ford built 1,000 replicas of the '76 Torino seen in the weekly police drama. The Dodge Chargers used in the television series *The Dukes of Hazard* is another good example. No one could have predicted that the 1962 Rambler American would become such a hot ticket item until it began to appear regularly on the sitcom *3rd Rock from the Sun*. As a result of exposure on network television, owners began to demand $5,000 and more for the rustiest of Rambler ragtops. Now they command upward of $14,000 for a prime example. Popularity is often luck of the draw.

# Some Models Are Almost Always Worth More Than Others

Fringe models almost always carry a higher value. These are convertibles, hardtops, and station wagons. Corresponding sedans are almost always lower in value unless they were manufactured in extremely limited numbers. Fun cars to watch out for are the 1969 Rambler Scrambler or the 1966 Ford Mustang High Country Special. Sold only in Colorado, Wyoming, and Nebraska, only 333 of these Mustangs were built. They could be had only in Timberline Green, Columbine Blue, or Aspen Gold. The High Country Specials returned in 1967 and 1968. Even more rare is the 1967 Ford Mustang Stallion. They carried special paint, Cougar taillights, and unique Stallion emblems. Only eight of these high-stepping ponies were let loose from the barn, and all were sold in Toronto.

The 1968 Ford Mustang High Country Special was one of 400 shipped to dealers in the Denver area.

A vehicle once owned by a celebrity is worth more than an ordinary one—if you have the papers to prove authenticity of ownership. A personal friend of mine owns the 1966 Rambler American 400 convertible presented to Miss Canada when she was crowned the most beautiful woman in the Dominion. Its value is a good bit higher than an ordinary Rambler American convertible built in the same year.

Actor Andy Griffith owned this 1935 Packard Four Door Convertible Sedan. It sold at the Kruse Labor Day Auction in 2005.

Listed as a "million dollar car," this 1968 Chevrolet Camaro went on the block at the 2005 Kruse Labor Day Auction.

## Don't Count Your Chickens!

The market value of your collectible car is always only what the public is willing to pay. I inherited my folks' 1963 Studebaker Lark Daytona Convertible. This car came loaded with absolutely every option possible, including the very rare factory air-conditioning. Each summer I would see a couple at a show in New York who offered to buy it because they already owned one and absolutely needed another to complete their matching "his-and-her" Lark set. Every winter they would ring up for a polite chat and inquire if I was interested in selling the Lark. The price went as high as $14,000, but I always refused their offer because I was—pardon the pun—having a lark with the pretty ragtop. When I was ready to sell in 1996, I called them, visions of an easy $14,000 already dancing in my bank account. I learned that the couple was in the middle of an ugly divorce and no longer interested. The bubble had burst and the market value was lowered. My beautiful Lark was sold for considerably less, but it found a home with very close friends who have kindly granted me permanent visiting rights to the Studebaker.

Chevrolets almost always carry a higher value than Fords and Plymouths built in the same year. Orphan makes such as Studebaker, Nash, Hudson, Kaiser, Frazer, and Willys often fetch less than their MoPar and Blue Oval counterparts. That doesn't dampen one's enjoyment, if those brands are meaningful to you, but they might not be the investment you seek. That hand-built, truly exotic 1954 Nash-Healey with body by Pinin Farina will draw huge crowds at shows, but a mass-produced Chevrolet Corvette from the same year is likely to have a higher book value.

Designed by Dutch Darrin, the 1954 Kaiser Darrin sports car with its fiberglass body can be had in the $42,500-price range. (Photo courtesy RM Auctions)

A couple of years ago, I received an e-mail from a bank manager in Alberta. As executor, he was attempting to settle the estate of a deceased client. Among the items to be liquidated was a pristine 1964 Rambler Classic with only 7,000 miles on the odometer. He had high hopes for its sale and needed an evaluation. Unfortunately, the 660 sedan had been garaged for more than two decades and required a fair amount of cosmetic work, rubber throughout, tires, and brakes. He was crushed to learn that the most he could expect for the car was south of the $3,000 mark.

## Cars Don't Always Hold Their Value

Tastes change over periods of time in the hobby. There is no guarantee that your purchase will continue to rise in value. There was a time when the 1959 Cadillac with its soaring fins fetched top dollar. Then the bubble burst. A new generation of collectors came along, a group not dazzled by the chrome and fins of the fifties because they did not remember those cars as being significant. Today the '59 Caddy is worth much less than it was 15 years ago. The Ford Model A is another example. My parents turned down $40,000 for their bright yellow Roadster in the 1980s. The generation that loved the Model A in its youth is rapidly dying off. When the folks' Ford did sell, it went for only half of what it did at the height of the craze.

At present, interest in traditional Classic cars is on the wane. The current generation of buyers is fascinated by muscle cars because those are the desirable cars of their youth. That market is changing, too. The best of the authentic muscle car market is drying up because the crème-de-la-crème of that genre is now in the hands of private collectors. It will regenerate in the future as these collectors sell their toys.

In the meantime a new market has emerged for older cars that have been technologically up-dated to meet the motoring requirements of the twenty-first century. More and more 1955

Chevrolets carry that stock look, but underneath the skin the vehicle bristles with total high-tech transformations. The updates include trick suspensions, leather interiors, the latest in sound systems, and four-wheel disc ABS brakes. While a 1967 Camaro is desirable, one that has been modified to meet the comfort needs of an ageing user is downright hot. At today's auctions we see more muscle cars cross the block with CD changers, new air-conditioning units, and many other convenience and comfort components.

A 1936 Cord Westchester is truly a work of art. The timeless Classic is worth serious consideration as an investment vehicle. (Photo courtesy of Kruse International)

## Know What You Are Buying

Please, please, please, do your homework so you know what you are buying. Don't believe everything you are told. Get tangible proof. The old Russian axiom warns one and all to "trust but verify." Wiser words were never spoken, no matter what the language. Save yourself Metric tons of heartache by being sure of your facts and then, like Santa's list, checking them twice. Auction houses require that sellers submit an accurate accounting and history of the vehicles that will roll onto the auction block but not all the consignees do this. Due diligence falls on the buyer.

Three years ago in Pennsylvania, I watched a gleaming 1955 Chevy Bel Air pull into a burger joint. Behind the wheel was a young U.S. marine. I walked across the parking lot to admire the beautiful two-tone Shadow Grey "Metalli-Chrome" over Coral paint job that adorned his gorgeous Bowtie. He proudly told me he had paid only $20,000 for the two-door hardtop. In fact, he had dropped his entire reenlistment bonus on his sweet investment. My heart sank. He hadn't bought a hardtop at all; this was an ordinary two-door sedan with a B-pillar sticking up between the doors, a big old B-pillar standing as tall as the Sears Tower. His lack of basic knowledge about automobile body styles had cost him a cool $10,000!

## Know What You Are Restoring

I offer this horror story to reinforce the fact that thorough homework is required before tackling a restoration project. One of the worst tales I have ever been told in my many years as an automotive historian involved a couple in Manitoba who discovered a 1958 Meteor Ranchero, squirreled away in a barn. The Meteor Ranchero was the Canada-only version of the Ford Ranchero, sold throughout the Dominion by Mercury-Meteor-Lincoln dealers. This is a highly uncommon pickup truck; only 138 of the sweet haulers were ever built. The couple did not belong to any clubs and never once thought to contact Ford of Canada for information, so they had no way of knowing that the 1958 Ranchero used the same cab, rear fenders, and taillight housing as the 1957 Meteor Rancheros. They carefully cut off the big round Full Circle Safety taillights and grafted on a pair from a 1958 Meteor station wagon. It was an enormous undertaking and turned out to be a huge mistake, one that lowered the value of their vehicle significantly.

Anxious to fill in the huge price gaps between Ford and Mercury, Ford of Canada created the Meteor. This badge-engineered car shared its body shell with Ford but was dressed very smartly in unique, upscale trim and swanky upholstery. It bowed to the public in April 1948 as a 1949 model. Meteor rocketed up to 23,027 sales in its first year on the market, giving it almost 11 percent of Canadian sales pie. The marque was discontinued in 1961 but was revived in 1965 for a second go at the market. The final year for the Canada-only member of the Blue Oval family was 1976.

# 5 TOOLS FOR EVALUATING A VEHICLE'S VALUE

## THE AUCTION CATALOG

The auction catalog is your primary tool for finding a vehicle that is appropriate to you and your lifestyle. This is a carefully annotated directory of all the vehicles to be offered on the auction date. Some are elaborate, elegant hardbound books, some are slick, glossy productions reminiscent of old Montgomery-Ward and Eaton's catalogs, while some catalogs will be as simple as a mimeographed list. Within its pages are pictures and descriptions of the vehicles that will appear on the block. Study it carefully. There is an index; use it! Don't be afraid to mark it up, write notes on it, circle the vehicles you would like to own, and dog-ear pages that are important to you.

Devouring the catalog before a sale is a great pleasure. A well-written catalog practically sells the automobiles. Each of the major houses does its utmost to make its catalogs as interesting and informative as possible. They are designed to plant the seeds of desire in your thoughts. Expect to read a fairly complete description of the vehicle. Sometimes the car's importance to automotive history is noted, and, occasionally, information about the automobile's history or even a little biography of the owner is included. Often an estimated value is included. Those vehicles marked as being offered with "no reserve" are guaranteed to sell on the auction date.

Kruse offers this well-detailed catalog for its spring Motorfest.

## Internet Sites

Used very much like the catalog, many of the auction houses have Web sites with images of the vehicles and what they sold for at the last auction. Barrett-Jackson's Web site gets 50 million hits a month, and on Auction Saturday alone, the site will register 350 million hits.

**Savvy Tip**

Photos of the vehicles being sold are supplied to the auction house by the sellers. The people at the auction house have no way of knowing when the picture was taken. Sometimes the images do not match the actual condition of the vehicle. Ask when the photo was taken. At one auction, the photo of a beautiful 1955 Chevrolet Bel Air Convertible was a billion light years away from matching the tired dog on the floor. When the discrepancy was pointed out the seller replied cheerily, "Oh! That picture was taken in 1980 when I bought it."

## Books and Periodicals

Do your research. Find out what your wheels are going to cost you. First, buy the latest issue of *Old Cars*, *Old Autos*, *Auto Week*, the *DuPont Registry*, or the *Auto Trader* for collectible vehicles. Check the national want ads to see what is on the market, in what conditions, and what price ranges. You will want to buy *Hemmings Motor News* and the latest edition of *Cars & Prices*, too. If you are looking for a truck, pick up *Double Clutch,* the *Wheels of Time*, and *Vintage Truck* magazine. Bring along your Blackberry and surf to the collectible car price guide sites. Arm yourself with as many fact sources as possible!

**Savvy Tip**

While *Vintage Truck* magazine is available at better bookstores and newsstands throughout the United States, *Double Clutch* and *Wheels of Time* are high quality periodicals that are the official club newsletters of the Antique Truck Club of America and the Antique Truck Historical Society, respectively. Their publications are available only by joining those organizations.

Over 72 car events listings and show & auction ads this week!

Vol. 35, No. 6, February 9, 2006

Old Cars

WEEKLY NEWS & MARKETPLACE

Check the news, expanded ad links and subscription offers at www.oldcarsweekly.com

GM Futurliner Tops Arizona Sales at $4 Million

By Keith Mathiowetz

At the mid-January collector car auctions in the Phoenix, Arizona, area, one special vehicle — a 1950 GM Futurliner Parade of Progress tour bus — sold for an amazing $4,000,000, the highest price paid for any vehicle among all the auctions that took place in the Grand Canyon State. The Futurliner is one of 12 self-contained display and transport vehicles created by General Motors and used in the company's Parade of Progress touring exhibits in the 1950s. It is also one of only three survivors restored to its original Parade of Progress configuration. The special tour bus is powered by a 400-cid GM truck engine and is fully equipped, including an onboard motor-generator and updated air conditioning for the driver's compartment.

For the general public to see a restored Futurliner was a rare event, but another one has been seen at select national shows for the last couple of years and will be on tour again this summer. At the Iola Old Car Show, which will take place July 7-9, 2006, in Iola, Wisconsin, Futurliner #10 will be on display for thousands of vintage car enthusiasts to enjoy in person. The 1953 vehicle, located in Zeeland, Michigan, is



*Old Cars* is one of the longest running periodicals in the collectible car hobby. It appears every week.

## Talk to People

Don't be in a hurry. Take a whole winter to determine asking prices. Take a summer, too. Do this by going to car shows and talking to people who have bought cars similar to the one you wish to own. Don't be too shy to ask consigners to show you receipts for the amount of work they have invested in their vehicles. They will usually be glad to do this but don't be miffed if they decline to show you the original bill of sale. Talk to collectors, dealers, professional old car appraisers, and even insurance adjusters. Check the information personally gathered against those published in the vintage car value guidebooks. The published car guide lists are reputable and claim to be accurate within 10 percent of the selling price. With all this information in hand, now you are ready to create that dream list.

If you know people in San Francisco, Tampa, or somewhere far from where you live, ask them to send you the collector car want ads out of the Sunday edition of their newspaper. Check your car club newsletter want ads, too. Track down rumors. I heard about a rare 1947 Nash half-ton pickup truck—only 22 were ever built—and traced it to France. Although the rare truck really did exist, it was not for sale.

Every truck owner's dream, this Nash pickup is one of only 22 ever built.

You've talked to folks in person, now you are ready to make telephone calls. You might need to call across the continent and further. Using the want ads, burn up the phone lines to Saskatchewan, South Carolina, Iowa, and Italy, if those are the places where your potential car awaits.

Ask questions about everything. Be sure to ask about conditions. If you learn that five of the 10 Oldsmobile 4-4-2s you dream of owning all have cracked blocks or the floor pans of those Renault Dauphines you want so badly are rusted completely through, consider carefully that this is possibly a design flaw or a manufacturing problem that you will have to deal with as the new owner. Subtract the estimated cost of repairs out of the price you are willing to pay.

In speaking directly to the owner, you can often get a feel for whether he or she appears to be trustworthy. Being exhaustive with your questions lets the seller know that you are thorough. Call a second time as follow-up to see if the seller is still singing the same tune. If the story changes, the car is very likely not what it is advertised to be.

With each conversation, take notes. Jot down the following information:

- Year
- Make
- Model
- Owner's name
- Owner's phone number
- Owner's mailing address
- Asking price
- Highest amount you are willing to spend
- Current established value of vehicle
- Condition and pertinent details

There are jewels in the rough, like this Packard, to be found virtually everywhere on this continent.

These notes you gather in each interview will be invaluable in helping you to narrow the field.

Even at auctions, not all cars that cross the block will be in pristine condition. Some are sold unrestored. A 1912 Rambler Gotham seven-passenger limousine went on the block at a recent auction. This stunning Brass Era example came from the Clarence Staab collection, liquidated at an estate sale held in Wisconsin in 2003. After decades of careless storage, the once elegant Rambler was in extremely sad condition.

Larry Finley was the auctioneer. He knows that a car like this doesn't come on the market very often. Once the advertising went out, calls poured into his office from all over the world, potential owners inquiring about the Rambler. Larry let them all know the condition. "It was all original but the car was a complete basket case," he told them. A family of raccoons had left countless muddy footprints all over the car, and proof of their presence was a half-eaten ear of corn on the seat in the limousine compartment. Larry scouted around the barn and unearthed the windows and even found the original hubs. The Rambler rested on John Deere tractor wheels.

"Despite its condition, it is the only Gotham in existence and one of only two Rambler limousines of that era left in existence," Larry told prospective buyers. The vehicle was complete and worth a fortune to someone willing to restore it to its former glory. The hammer price for this rare, if rough, Brass Era treasure was $32,500. The car is undergoing restoration.

### The Story Behind the Deal

David Hansen of Berwyn, Illinois, saw the ad for the 1912 Rambler Gotham in *Hemmings Moter News*. He went up to Wisconsin to eyeball the car. The auctioneer was accommodating; he even pulled the vehicle out of the barn for David to examine. The wood framing used in the body was still in excellent shape. The interior was completely intact, though the electric intercom between the passenger compartment and the chauffeur was missing. David knew instinctively that this example would go for between $25,000 and $30,000. He wisely shot a whole roll of film and sent the pictures to several Brass Era experts for their learned opinions. David already owned a 1903 Rambler Runabout and a 1913 Rambler Cross-Country Touring Car. He needed a third for the collection. He admits to being a little nervous about his chances of acquiring the Gotham because a famous collector was rumored to be interested.

On auction day, he watched the crowd carefully. Most could be dismissed as serious competition because they didn't even know what they were looking at. David heard more than one express the opinion that the Rambler had to be British because it featured right-hand drive. Uninformed comments like that made him feel a little more confident. Bidding opened at $25,000 because a sealed bid had come in to the auction house for that amount. The auctioneer told the crowd that if there were no higher bids the car was sold. Someone in the audience promptly raised the price to $27,500. David bought the 1912 Rambler Gotham on the third bid. He was very surprised at his acquisition.

His first issue was that the 7 foot-eight-inch tall car did not fit in the garage he had prepared for the limousine. He wound up storing it in a friend's airport hanger. David has spent time looking for missing parts like headlights and the opera lights at the top of the roof. Other lights were in bad shape. All of the nuts and bolts simply crumble at the sight of a wrench or screwdriver because the car sat in storage since 1941. They will all have to be machined. David surmises that the missing headlights and wheel rims were probably scooped up in a scrap drive during World War II and made into weapons of war.

As a member of the Horseless Carriage Club of America, he has an excellent network for restoration tips and parts at his disposal. Often someone with a similar vehicle is willing to loan a part so that it can be duplicated.

David's goal is to show the Rambler Gotham at Hershey and compete. His advice is to get to an auction early so you can get in synch with the auctioneer's patter and actions. Auctioneers often point at the person who is expected to make the next bid and David was never quite sure if the auctioneer was pointing at him or not.

A couple I know undertook the restoration of a one-of-a-kind wooden-bodied station wagon from the 1930s. Twenty years and more than $200,000 later, they have a magnificent, historic vehicle of which they are truly proud. I, however, have reached a time in life where I prefer a turnkey car to a fixer-upper. That's an individual decision we each have to make.

## Vehicle Condition Scales

As a collector, you will become familiar with vehicle condition scales. There are several, all developed by competitors in the old car industry. However, they all rank the quality of a vehicle's state into four, five, or six categories, based on the condition of the body, interior, drive train, and chassis. If someone tells you that the GTO you want is rated as being Condition Three, according to *Cars & Prices*, make sure you have the book on hand so you can follow along!

A car that is "like showroom new" is considered to be in excellent condition. It is a given that this vehicle is not driven, only shown. Folks who drive their cars regularly for pleasure refer to these perfect glamour girls as "trailer queens."

The 1961 Ford Thunderbird is a car that is often overrestored.

Some vehicles are overrestored, that is, the cars are actually better now than when they rolled out of the factory doors. The 1961 crop of Ford Thunderbirds all left the factory in Wixom, Michigan, with a nasty little "lip" on the passenger's side doorsill that many restorers would simply grind off. Over restoration is a mistake that has cost many an unsuspecting owner valuable points at judging time because each and every coveted point is awarded for factory authenticity, not restorer's perfection.

A little south of the 100-point show cars are carefully cared-for original vehicles or superbly restored cars that show only slight wear. These examples are considered to be in very good to fine condition. This would be the equivalent of a car that has been on the road for a couple of years but has been scrupulously maintained.

If the vehicle is drivable "as is" or needs only minor repairs before running the roads, then it is considered to be in good condition. It may need restoration but it is complete. I laid down $35 for a perfectly good 1965 Fiat Spyder in Indiana. It was cheap because the transmission was shot. The repair cost me $100 and I tooled around in a fun set of wheels.

A restorable car is one that is completely intact but needs a total restoration. Some lucky boys I know stumbled across a 1966 Marlin Tahiti in a barn in Pennsylvania. The Tahiti was a one-off prototype put to work on the show car circuit to drum up interest in American Motors' products. The Marlin was a total mess but worth every penny to the boys that discovered it. They will restore it, right down to the brightly patterned South Seas upholstery. Restoring a prototype can bring special headaches because the car was meant for show, not to drive. The Tahiti had clay door handles and window rollers inside that crumbled when touched. They had to be fabricated by hand, using pictures as a guide. Not everyone can brag that the car you're drooling over is "one of only one ever built!"

Some cars are scrapped and then stripped to the point where they are beyond the point of restoration. They are often, however, still good for parts. These rusty, picked-over hulks are not to be sniffed at; you may find yourself in seventh heaven if you are lucky enough to find one. It may well yield up some terrific parts, especially those oh-so-hard to find trim pieces.

I spent three years looking for the brightwork to bolt onto the passenger side of my 1966 Dodge Coronet 500 four-door sedan. I finally located them in Aroostook County, Maine, but the owner was in a mood. He wouldn't sell me the parts I wanted; I had to buy the whole darned Dodge and drag it out of a swampy forest filled with black spruce and black flies. Those precious trim pieces made it worth every painful black fly bite!

Savvy Tip

Not all improvements you choose to make to your vehicle will increase its value. I treated myself to a set of factory correct Kelsey-Hayes mag wheels for my 1969 AMC Ambassador wagon. They certainly dressed up the package, but at sale time my $1,000 purchase did not add appreciably to the price.

American Motors flagship was the Ambassador. The 1969 DPL Wagon appealed to buyers who sought value. (Photo courtesy of Elton McFall)

## The Wow! Factor

In considering the balance between enjoyment and investment this is the perfect place to introduce the Wow! Factor. It is the measurable, visible pleasure that your car brings to others. Every million-dollar moment of pleasure with a collector car comes from the appreciation and homage that someone has paid to your wheels.

Frank Pigeon lives in Montreal. He is on the Mayor's List of people to call when hot collectible cars are needed at events to raise money for worthy causes. The mayor wants cars that draw crowds and make people say "Wow!" when they see them. Frank will roar into the appointed venue behind the wheel of his bright red 1969 AMX. Being a modest man, he likes to joke that his racy two-seater sports car "is just a fast Rambler." This offering from American Motors is so seldom seen by the public it consistently draws more folks to its side than the fancy Ferraris and the Lamborghinis flanking Frank's pride and joy.

The AMX is a seldom-seen sports car. The two-seater was introduced by American Motors for the 1968 season and withdrawn at the end of the 1970 model year.

I once owned a lowly 1963 Studebaker Standard. This car was such a stripper it sold for $1,800 new including the taxes and two mounted snow tires. I know, because it belonged to my very frugal grandmother, who died with the first nickel she ever made firmly glued to the bottom of her pocket book. This car had not a bit of chrome on it; it was such a Plain Jane that it didn't even have the fancy flip-top Vanity glove box with the pop-up makeup mirror, just a cardboard flap. I never did restore the car, just drove it as it was, faded blue paint and all. Despite its well-worn look, the little Studebaker was a head turner.

Parked next to my Studebaker at one show, was a perfect, 100-point, flame-orange 1954 Cadillac convertible, replete with white leather interior. A rock star owned it. Throughout the day folks flocked to look at the starkly humble stripper, barely noticing the magnificent Caddy. They were full of questions about the unusual looking little Studebaker. Finally, the exasperated singer turned to me. "I don't get it," he sputtered. "I spent a fortune on this Caddy, won all kinds of prizes with it, and no one is spending time drooling over it, today. They're all over your Studebaker, and it isn't even restored." I commiserated with him, explained that people are drawn to the weird, the unknown, and the unusual. That day we watched the Wow! Factor at work firsthand.

The 1952 Nash Rambler was opulent. Dressed with a radio, heater, white wall tires, leather trimmed seats as standard equipment it cost $17 more than a stripped Chevy.

A couple I know owns a 1952 Nash Rambler. While on a trip, they stopped at a plaza in New Jersey to fill up with gas. A woman in a new Chevrolet Suburban pulled up alongside. She climbed down from her vehicle and walked over to the little Nash Rambler. She didn't even say "Hello!" to the folks at the pump. Instead, she began to serenade them with "Beep Beep," the kitschy but catchy song recorded by the Playmates in 1958. They crooned the tale of a little Nash Rambler that passed a mighty Cadillac in second gear. When the lady was done singing, she bowed low and walked away. "It was a million-dollar moment," the couple remembers.

The 1954 Cadillac is popular with collectors.

Pure homage is what the Wow! Factor is all about and that will mean a lot whether you drive your dream down to the Freeze Queen on Friday evenings or watch the investment rise on paper while it sits in climate-controlled storage. The choice is yours to make.

**Meet Craig and Alane Grosz — Collectors**

Craig Grosz is one of the hobby's important collectors. He was born and grew up in Wahpeton, North Dakota, where his dad, William, was a pharmacist. Craig's love affair with cars started very early. His first recollection is of a 1960 Thunderbird, his dad's first new car. Now, a Thunderbird was very flashy for North Dakota and almost not "Christian" by many accounts. That car was the talk of the town. The four-seater was certainly impractical for a family of five. His mother would let him play in the car for hours on end. He was fascinated with the cockpit interior. He marveled at the perforated headliner and had to be reminded constantly not to touch it.

The Thunderbird was not the kind of car that good citizens in North Dakota bought. William's father badgered him to buy a proper car. Finally the exotic bird was sold, and the Grosz family was seen in a sensible Buick sedan. No doubt the whole town heaved a sigh of relief.

Craig and his brother, Richard, and his sister, Rebecca, all learned to drive in a used 1964 Mercury Monterrey. Their dad figured it was big, heavy, and safe. The Merc suffered its share of dings at the hands of its teenaged owners. Richard backed into somebody, but Craig hit someone head-on. Fortunately, it was nothing more than a big fender bender. While goofing around with friends, someone put the car into reverse and tore the door off as it hit the side of the garage. Needless to say, the poor Mercury spent a lot of time in the shop.

*1953 Corvette #186 is Craig's favorite fast bowtie.*

Craig bought a red 1964 Ford F-150 when he was a junior in high school. It cost him $1,100. He paid cash with money earned working at the family drugstore. Dad approved of the purchase and bought a topper. The 17-year-old had bigger aspirations than a lowly pickup. He sold the Ford, took the cash to the bank, and wanted to borrow an additional $2,200. The bank approved since his dad was on its board of directors. The loans officer figured the kid was good for it. Craig's dad turned out to be furious at the loans officer for signing a contract with a minor.

Craig bought a used medium blue metallic 1970 Mustang Mach 1 with the 428 Cobra Jet setup. The interior was black. The car lasted all spring and summer, but it needed three clutches during that short time in Craig's hands. The local Ford dealer didn't buy Craig's story that the clutches were defective. He paid for the first one out of his own pocket and borrowed the money for the other two from his sister. He paid Rebecca back, but it was a secret. His parents don't know about the loans to this day. Well, they will find out when they read this story. Back to ordinary wheels, Craig finished high school in a mundane Ford Falcon that he barely remembers.

*Craig enjoys working on his cars. He's under the hood of his 1954 Chevrolet Corvette.*

*Craig bought this 1970 Ford Mustang Mach 1 with the 428 mill and the Ram Air option because it was like the one he owned in high school.*

With diploma in hand, Craig attended the North Dakota State School of Science in Wahpeton for a year. School didn't turn his crank, and the teenager found himself at loose ends. He moved to Minneapolis to work for his uncle at his office supply store. Uncle Paul was a car nut. The two of them attended a collector car auction, Craig's first. They didn't buy anything, but Craig got the auction bug. The memory of that excitement never left him.

Later, Uncle Paul and Craig went to a car restorer, and Craig bought a 1960 Corvette for $4,200. The car did not sport factory paint; it was head-turning green metallic. Nine months later it was sold, and a blue ragtop 1969 Corvette with the 427-cubic-inch engine was purchased.

*Here is one of Craig's 1953 Corvettes. Car #120 was featured in* Hemmings.

Craig then went to work for Benson Optical in the Twin Cities as an optician-trainee and got his optician's certification. Then he transferred to Benson Optical in Traverse City, Michigan. The 'Vette went with him. While he was there, he met and married Rebecca Frederick, and soon, son Justin joined the family. The marriage didn't go so well, and the couple parted. Craig struggled to make ends meet and put aside his passion for cars to meet the obligations of daily life. He moved back to the Twin Cities in 1981.

Success was an easy ladder to climb because Craig was putting in 60 to 70 hours a week as a vice president in the optical business. He met Alane Schlecht a year later. Realizing he had found a true soul mate, they got married and daughter Cassidy came along in 1983. Partners in life, they share many passions including a genuine love for antique cars. Craig never buys without laying out a game plan for Alane's input and approval.

*Craig and Alane's first Corvette was purchased on June 1, 1989, Alane's birthday. Alane got to drive the 1973 Stingray.*

All this time Craig had the itch to own another vintage set of speedy wheels. Finally, on June 1, 1989—Alane's birthday—he got back into cars in a very tangible way. Craig had saved up $10,000 in cash for a 1973 Corvette silver and black with black interior. He and Alane went to look at it. Alane guarded the savings and negotiated the deal. When she pulled out the stack of $100 bills, the owner drooled and took it, dropping the price by a cool $5,000. Craig gave Alane the best birthday present ever—a "heck of a good ride in the car." He chuckles, "I even let her drive it."

*This 1957 Chevrolet Bel Air convertible was the first car that Craig and Alane sold at Cox's Auction in Branson, Missouri.*

That Corvette was the first in Craig's current collection. The family went to Mesa, Arizona, in 1994, and Craig and Alane attended the Barrett-Jackson auction. He heard about the event from his dad and decided to check it out. Wisely, they went as observers that first year but got a real good taste for how the event worked. They saw cars selling in the $40,000 to $60,000 range. Alane told her husband, "Don't think you're going to bid in the $100,000 range." That was then. Now they routinely bid and buy in that higher range. Craig recalls that his first $100,000 purchase made his knees shake with anticipation.

*Craig bought this 1963 Corvette roadster at the Mid-America Auction in the Twin Cities.*

Craig immediately got caught up in the auction fever. "It was like being in a candy store. I start out with one car in mind, and then all those other cars show up. I can talk to the owners and don't have to travel all over God's green acres to see one." His wife enjoys the show as well and has no interest in the lifestyle pavilions. They have invested in a motor home in order to be comfortable in their pursuit of the collector car dream. Hitched to the motor home is a 24-foot trailer in case they decide to bring home a vehicle.

*Craig and Alane's 1960 Ford Thunderbird carries the 430-cubic-inch Lincoln motor.*

Craig surprised his dad one Christmas with this 1948 Studebaker President Land Cruiser.

After that, he checked out Kruse in Indiana and some of the MidAmerica Auctions in the Twin Cities. They returned to Barrett-Jackson and started adding to the collection.

Tired of the long hours and the time away from family, Craig decided to get out of the corporate world and open an auto repair store. With time, he owned three and sold them in 2001. He retired at 45 to have fun.

Craig had always believed that collector cars were solid investments. He had a tough row to hoe in order to convince his wife and his dad that wheels were good investments. After they attended an auction with Craig, they were convinced that he was right on the money and gave him the green light to indulge his passion. They came home from the auction with a 1957 Chevrolet Bel Air convertible, the real McCoy and a red one to boot.

*Craig takes the 1972 Corvette Stingray to a car show.*

An article about Jim Cox's auction in *Sports Car Marketplace* made him decide to add Branson, Missouri, to the itinerary. He called Jim Cox and was immediately impressed at the personal touch and the time he took to chat with Craig. That really made Craig and Alane hungry to make the 1,000-mile trek. They hauled the '57 Bel Air to Branson and got their asking price. The auction wasn't the only fun in town; the shows and live entertainment in Branson was right up the family's alley, suiting their Christian values. Craig notes with satisfaction that they have sold five cars at the Cox Auction—always getting their price. They are pleased with the two cars they have purchased in Branson, as well.

*Craig and Alane own this 1967 Corvette coupe.*

Craig used to be a pilot and owned four airplanes. He even built a home on an airpark and erected a hangar in the backyard. The family had no passion or interest in aviation

*Craig and Alane sold this 1968 Ford Shelby GT 500 KR at the Branson Auction in October 2005.*

or even flying. Craig came to realize that his time with planes was solitary and that he was cutting himself out of quality time with the family. He made a decision to abandon the hobby and refocus his energies on an activity that the whole family could enjoy. Everybody in the Grosz household took to antique cars like Minnesota ducks take to the state's 10,000 lakes.

Craig enjoys investing time and money into the restoration of a car so that it is even better than when new. Craig and Alane both feel that they are not just restoring a car; they are preserving a part of America's history. That is the very root of their passion. They only invest in cars that have histories behind them. That boils down to vehicles from the muscle car era. In the late 1960s, a buyer could walk into a dealership and option out a vehicle to personal specs. The right combination gave the new owner a car that could be driven from the showroom straight to the track for racing. The build sheet and the bill of sale give it its authenticity.

*The 1969 Chevrolet Z-28 RS is a favorite at car shows.*

The last car they sold was a 1968 Mustang GT500 KR. It went for $137,000. From an investment standpoint, Craig and Alane were $35,000 to the good on the deal. They don't count labor or travel time and expenses; that's part of the passion. When it happens that an even more desirable vehicle comes along that Craig must have, he and his wife sit down and decide which car will go on the block. He admits that there is anxiety in parting with a vehicle. Fortunately, Alane is big on scrapbooking, and they both enjoy rumbling through the albums to remember cars they owned and put their imprint on.

*Craig and Alane's 1965 Corvette.*

Craig and Alane keep their babies in heated storage. There are two 1953 Corvettes, a 1965 Corvette roadster with the L78 engine option, a 1967 Corvette with the L36 mill. There is a pair of 1969 Corvettes, one with the L46 engine and the other powered by the L36 mill. In addition, there is a 1970

Mustang Mach 1 with the 428 engine and Ram Air induction. Next in the lineup is a 1969 Camaro Z-28 RS, a 1960 Ford Thunderbird ragtop with factory air-conditioning and genuine leather upholstery. The Squarebird sports the 430-cubic-inch Lincoln motor—rare because only 220 were built.

Also included is the 1948 Studebaker President exactly like Craig's grandfather owned, his first new car. The swanky Studebaker was a Christmas present from Craig to his dad. William recalls he was 17 when he and his father went to the dealer to pick up the shiny new Studebaker with the suicide doors. Today, his dad drives the South Bend beauty on occasion, and it is his pride and joy.

Craig has just refurbished a 1953 Corvette that was featured in *Hemmings Motor News.* These vintage cars are part of the legacy that he and Alane will leave to their children. They will be passionate about the hobby forever and have instilled that love in the next generation. Craig admits to having a favorite; he could live without all of his cars except for the 1953 Corvette. He is only the third owner. It is car #186 to roll out the factory doors.

---

Harley Earl was vice president of General Motors Art & Colour Section. He noted that his son was crazy about the post-war MGs that hit the American market. Earl decided that Chevrolet should mass-produce a two-seater for the U.S. market. The Corvette debuted for the 1953 season. Actor John Wayne was photographed with one of the first Corvettes, and the market was targeted to celebrities and folks belonging to the well-heeled golf club set. Initially the Corvette did not sell well. Management was ready to pull the plug on the fiberglass sports car. Ironically, it was Ford that rescued the Corvette from oblivion with its introduction of the Thunderbird for the 1955 model year.

---

# 6 SO MANY KINDS, SO MANY PLAYERS!

## AUCTIONS ARE AS OLD AS THE HILLS

Auctions have been around practically as long as civilization itself. Some historians contend that the sale of Joseph's coat of many colors, a transaction recorded in the Book of Genesis, was the very first auction. Regardless of when it all started, the tradition of public buying and selling in front of an audience has stood the test of time as a valid form of commerce and still draws millions.

The first documented auction in secular history took place in 500 B.C.E. in Babylon. By law, all single women in the realm were ordered to stand for marriage auctions once a year. Prospective brides were sold to the highest bidders. While beautiful women sold as fast as pancakes at a Shrove Tuesday dinner, plain women augmented their chances of saying "I do!" by standing on the auction block with dowries that included gold, precious jewels, land, and valuable livestock, all to entice bidders.

# Auction Houses

The thrill of the hunt, the rhythmic chant of the auctioneers, and the excitement of bidding all generate a level of enthusiasm that only the auction method of marketing can inspire in a crowd. You are about to discover that excitement for yourself!

Some of these auctions offer far more than the sale of goods. A number of them have grown into spectacular lifestyle affairs and are absolutely enormous in size. They hold all the excitement of Las Vegas, the Super Bowl, the Stanley Cup, and the World Series, all rolled into one electrically charged, carnival-like atmosphere. The auction drama is real, bidders get right up on the stage and play against sports legends and Hollywood stars, every one of them fixated on the prize, keen to go home with a set of dream wheels.

Held each January in Scottsdale, Arizona, the Barrett-Jackson extravaganza draws nearly 250,000 people. More than 4,000 of those in attendance participate in the auction. Ordinary folks rub shoulders with some of the biggest Hollywood stars, all pumped and primed to be the highest bidder. Surprisingly, 40 percent of the bidders are first-timers in the 315-foot wide by 390-foot long tent, identified by one of the largest American flags in existence.

To show its support for our troops, all American and Canadian soldiers who come to Barrett-Jackson in uniform are admitted at no charge.

More than a million folks sit in the comfort of their homes glued to the 24-hour Barrett-Jackson auction on the Speed network. Television coverage has catapulted the auction into an upscale lifestyle event and an essential part of the "must do" social scene. Being televised, the event has educated women to the pleasure of auctions and the proportional increase of women who bid is directly tied to television. Barrett-Jackson has grown to include an automobile pavilion and a complete lifestyle pavilion where many of the ladies opt to hang out. There they can enjoy the designer fashion show, get a soothing massage, have a Botox treatment, and purchase high-end jewelry. The art gala at Barrett- Jackson's Scottsdale event draws 8,000 connoisseurs.

Many who participate in the Barrett-Jackson event will be on hand for the Russo & Steele (RM Auctions, Inc.) auction in nearby Phoenix, held only a few days later. Russo & Steele also hails from Scottsdale, Arizona. Its event is held at the same time as the Barrett-Jackson gala at the Scottsdale Airport. Muscle cars, higher end muscle and sports cars, Shelbys, and special order COPO Chevrolets are the specialty of Russo & Steele.

The Kruse gathering in Auburn, Indiana, attracts approximately 300,000 spectators at its 480-acre home. This event is pure homespun midwestern pleasure, and the company behind it is billed as the world's largest collector car sales organization. The Kruse auction was televised for the first time in 2004. During the weeklong Hoosierland event, held annually during the week of Labor Day, the auctioneer's hammer comes down on approximately 5,000 collectible cars. The auction event is not the only thing in town, the Auburn Cord Duesenberg Festival is held every year in conjunction with the auction park's extravaganza. There is the thrilling Parade of Classics, featuring what else, but Auburns, Cords, and Duesenbergs; each magnificent motorcar is guaranteed to send shivers up and down your spine as it roars past.

The Labor Day week is truly a celebration of all things midwestern, boasting an antique show, an arts and crafts show, a quilting show, a hot air balloon event, even a showcase home decorated by top professionals in the field. There are several automobile and truck museums to visit, and you haven't lived until you have feasted on traditional Hoosier cuisine. If you can't make it back home to Indiana, Kruse holds events in Texas, Arizona, and Florida, too.

While trucks do cross the auction block at the big auction extravaganzas, the actual percentage of haulers runs only around five percent of the total vehicles auctioned. Most of these have been customized. This may not be the ideal venue for purchasing a truck.

Now that you have made up your mind to sample the auction experience and even possibly purchase a collectible vehicle at one, it is important to determine what kind of auction venue suits you best. Auction types vary widely and the major categories are listed here.

## Event and Gala Auctions

Barrett-Jackson, Kruse International, and RM Auctions, Inc. are among the biggest players in North America. Bonham & Brooks is a highly respected house from Britain that visits our side of the Atlantic. Well known and well publicized, each firm has a long history as classic and collectible auto auctioneers. These premier houses offer a full schedule of auction events held on different parts of the continent throughout the calendar year. Consult their Web sites for details: (www.barrett-jackson.com, www.kruseinternational.com, www.rmauctions.com, and www.bonhams.com).

Associated with all of these first-tier auction houses are some of the most prestigious collectible vehicle auctions in the world. The mere mention of Pebble Beach or Meadow Brook conjures up images of beautiful people in posh settings, surrounded by elegant, exotic classic motorcars.

These firms do far more than auction off cars to the highest bidder. Because they understand the intimate nature of the auction and the passion it arouses, what they provide at their premier events is immersion in a totally sensual consumer experience. Every moment at a gala auction event has been painstakingly designed to captivate and delight the senses. Guests who participate in these festive occasions receive careful, special, personal attention from the staff members. The attention to detail keeps them coming back for more.

At gala and event auctions, those who take part become members of a very elite community. While the auction is the anchor event, it is only part of a much larger package. There is the magnificent Concours d'Elegance, where owners showcase their wheels. There is golf, junkets to nearby historic sites, cocktail gatherings, fashion shows, high-end shopping excursions, guest speakers, and entertainment. Proceeds from the banquets benefit worthy causes or charities. Often these dinners are formal, black tie affairs. All of these functions lead up to the actual auction where millions are spent on classic and rare collectible vehicles.

Each of the major houses supports one or more worthy causes. Child Help is the charity of choice for Barrett-Jackson, and in 2005 the nonprofit organization received $2 million from the auction house.

## Mainstream Auctions

The big houses do not only auction off classic cars but also boast a complete line of what is known in the industry as mainstream auctions. These events carry specific names that let you know if the featured wheels to be sold are muscle cars, hot rods, sports cars, or collectible vehicles from various eras. Less formal than the prestigious gala auctions, these events generate their own brand of excitement.

You can leave the tuxedo at home if you plan to attend a mainstream auction; dress for these occasions is business casual.

## Government and Police Auctions

When criminals are convicted, their ill-gotten gains are seized by the police and sold to the public at auctions. Their goods are confiscated because these individuals have broken trade regulations, violated trademark or copyright laws, engaged in smuggling, drug trafficking, money laundering, credit card fraud, welfare fraud, mail fraud, or some other illegal activity. Before the auction takes place, all liens are cleared.

The practice of selling the proceeds seized as a result of criminal activity was expanded greatly in the United States when Congress passed the Comprehensive Crime Control Act in 1984. This law authorizes the sale of illegally obtained items or items obtained with illegal money to be sold and the profit put back into law enforcement agencies. Public auctions are the designated method of disposal. The auction house responsible for carrying out this task is the privately owned and operated Federal Assets Recovery Service.

While the sole purpose of these auctions is to dispose of forfeited and surplus goods and not at all geared to collector vehicles, collectible cars do turn up with surprising regularity. Notices of upcoming auctions are published in leading newspapers. One is wise to check Internet Web sites for online auction times and dates, too.

The Drug Enforcement Agency (DEA) sells seized vehicles on a regular basis. At the time of this writing, the DEA acts as an auction agent for 20 different American government agencies and departments. In addition to the DEA, some federal departments arrange auctions of their own. Those in the latter category include the U.S. Treasury, the Internal Revenue Service, and U.S. Customs.

Vehicles seized by U.S. Customs are sold in Miami and Fort Lauderdale, Florida; Edison, New Jersey; Edinburg, El Paso, and Laredo, Texas; Nogales, Arizona; San Diego, California; and San Juan, Puerto Rico.

Packard's prestige was fading by 1950 but this Touring Sedan still carried all the hallmarks of elegance.

One day, at a major U.S.-Canada border crossing, I couldn't help but admire the big, old, beautiful Mercedes-Benz ahead of me. From where I sat, I noted that its occupants seemed nervous and were acting oddly. Eventually the Mercedes pulled up to the kiosk. The Customs Officer examined the occupants' passports and asked a number of questions. It was a long wait, and finally I shut off my engine. At one point, the officer asked the driver to open the trunk. To my utter astonishment, the trunk of that Mercedes was absolutely stuffed to overflowing with loose greenbacks! The pair was immediately pulled out of the car and taken inside the building for questioning. The Mercedes was impounded and towed away. If they were found guilty of anything, dollars to doughnuts that lovely Mercedes would have wound up on the auction block.

Police in some major American cities also auction off seized automobiles, while others send their vehicles to the DEA. Boston and New York City hold auctions; at the time of publication, San Diego does not. More and more seized cars are being sold through Sheriffs' auctions, as well.

There is always the possibility that you will attend one of these auctions with the intention of buying a 1967 Mercury Cougar and come home with a case of Glenfiddich single malt whisky, three full-length black sable coats, and one slightly used NASA communications satellite, as well. Don't think I'm kidding about the satellite, either.

The Mercury Cougar was introduced for the 1967 model year. A Dan Gurney special, with performance options, appeared quickly.

From Alabama to Wyoming, all 50 state governments hold periodic auctions. Some states have the additional responsibility of selling off the surpluses of the federal agencies located within their borders. Alabama not only holds public auctions, the Yellowhammer State has sealed bid auctions, too.

If the 50 states are not exotic enough for you, there are also auctions in each of the U.S.-held territories and possessions. You can plan a holiday to the Commonwealth of Puerto Rico, home to 25 annual government auctions, or take a trip to Guam where 21 auctions are held each year.

## Auctions in Canada

In Canada, the police also seize goods and vehicles proven to be the profit of any criminal activity. Government-seized vehicles are auctioned off through the Crown Assets Distribution Centres, located across the country. This agency is a Crown (government owned) corporation, operating under the mandate of the federal Ministry of Public Works and Government Services.

All police departments in major Canadian cities hold auctions, as do the Royal Canadian Mounted Police (RCMP), the Ontario Provincial Police (OPP), and the Surete du Quebec, a.k.a. the Quebec Provincial Police.

Auctions in *la Belle Province* are conducted in French, although I have attended auctions in Quebec that were conducted simultaneously in French and English, a considerable talent on the part of the bilingual auctioneer!

## Importing a Collectible Car

Should you purchase a vehicle outside of the country, it must conform to the laws of the land into which you intend to import it. Regulations vary greatly, depending on the make, model, and year of manufacture of the vehicle. Check with U.S. Customs or Canada Customs about the regulations appropriate to the vehicle you wish to import. Some states and provinces require a letter from the police in the jurisdiction of purchase that indicates the vehicle has not been stolen. Be prepared to pay any applicable duty and sales taxes. Major credit cards are accepted for such payments.

The general rule of thumb for importation of a vehicle is that if it is 25 years or older, it is exempt from duty. Taxes will still have to be paid, as will any other fees and charges deemed appropriate by Customs. Call Customs for information pertinent to your vehicle before you import.

Savvy Tip

Rules and regulations concerning the importation of vehicles change frequently, and the officer you speak to may not have the latest information. Call Customs on different days, at different times of day, in different cities if necessary, and ask the same questions. When you hear the same answers three times, you can be reasonably sure the information is current.

A couple I know bought a vintage motor home (yes, there are dedicated fans and a thriving market for those, too!) in Florida, for a song, at an estate auction. They had no idea whatsoever that their new purchase did not conform to the regulations of Canada's Ministry of Transport (MOT), and they were denied permission to import their prize. It took a long time to sell, and they were naturally unhappy about their experience. They could have consulted with the MOT before buying and saved themselves a great deal of money and grief. If there is the slightest bit of doubt, check it out!

Savvy Tip

Don't waste money to join a commercial auction site on the Internet. These services charge $35 to $70 to advise you of upcoming government auctions. The agencies that handle government auctions charge only from $1 to $5 to register and, once on their mailing list, will advise you as to future sales events without any charge at all. That modest fee paid to the agency gets you a password, so that you can go online and view images of the items to be sold. If a physical catalog is desired, there is another small fee to cover shipping costs.

## Bankruptcy Auctions

Bankruptcies and estates without beneficiaries will also yield up automotive treasures as governments attempt to recoup revenue. Sometimes those surplus items include collectible cars. As is the case with all other government-sponsored auctions, all vehicles are cleared of any outstanding liens before the sale takes place.

## Private Estate Auctions

When people die, often their heirs would rather have the money than the goods willed to them. Auction firms are old, reliable hands, experienced at liquidating estates. Announcements are placed in local newspapers to alert the public to an impending sale date. It is quite common to see these announcements on local cable television stations, too.

If it is a large estate with many items to be sold, there may be a catalog. This can range from a simple typed list to an elaborate book with descriptions and even color pictures. Regardless of whether there is a catalog or not, there will be a preview period when prospective bidders can physically inspect the lots that will be sold.

Rarely are things sold separately. Items are often grouped together in lots to keep the action lively and make the auction move more quickly. Sometimes similar items, such as old car sales brochures, antique tools, or tractor repair manuals will be sold in a single lot. You may only want the 1940 Hupmobile service manual but find yourself bidding on 50 years' worth of old phone books and the hand-crank wall phone included in that lot, in order to get what you want. When a lot is up for bids, the auctioneer will say, "All for one money." This indicates that everything in the box, the lot, or the row is included in the winning bid.

Very often you can turn right around and sell the unwanted items to someone who was bidding against you because they are keen to own the old phone books and the hand-crank wall phone and don't give a flying fox about the Hupmobile manual. Similarly, if you aren't the highest bidder, it is perfectly acceptable auction etiquette to approach the individual who was successful and ask if that Hupmobile manual is for resale.

Often there are collectible vehicles to be had at estate auctions. If one appeals to you, speak to the auction staff and inquire as to who the car's regular mechanic was. Arrange a chat with the mechanic. At an auction preview, you will be allowed to start the vehicle but don't expect to be allowed to drive it.

Weekend auctions tend to draw larger crowds. Your chances for paying a lower price is better at auctions held on weekdays.

# Farm Auctions

Sadly, farm auctions are dwindling in number. These auctions are held for numerous reasons including death, no heirs to inherit, retirement, poor health, and being too close to a growing urban area, just to name a few. Whatever the reason, farm auctions are almost always mind-boggling in their diversity because farmers seldom, if ever, throw anything—and I do mean anything—away.

At my parents' farm auction, three sale dates were spread over a six-week period, right after harvest. Farm auctions are complex, to say the least. Depression Glass was being sold on the front lawn at the same time the antique tools were auctioned off in the shed, while at a third venue on the back porch, interested parties crowded around the auctioneer to bid on the vintage baseball card collection.

Ever thrifty, the folks never discarded anything. Literally everything they ever owned was recycled. When their 1928 Essex was no longer roadworthy, the elderly sedan was given a second life as a chicken coop. Those lucky hens laid a lot of eggs in a fine automobile through the years. The Essex was absolutely filthy but completely intact, and to my surprise, the closed sedan sold for a pretty penny at the auction.

Hopeful buyers descended on the farm from the four corners of the earth after spotting the advertisement that appeared in a national antique car club magazine. The old car auction was an all-day affair. The hammer dropped more than 200 times on the vehicles that crossed the block. Cars and trucks being sold ranged from rusted hulks dating back to the 1920s and 1930s

A nice 1948 Studebaker two-ton stake bed truck may very well surprise you at an auction one day.

to a 60-year-old Studebaker two-ton stake bed truck in good working order, some truly odd German bubble cars that had caught the folks' fancy, right up to a number of near perfect Milestone vehicles.

What was left of a trio of 1962 Chevrolet Corvair Monza Spyders went for $200 while a "his-and-her" set of matching 1957 Lincoln Premieres fetched a very handsome price. Every vehicle was sold "as is."

Savvy Tip

Dress casually for a farm auction. Wear plenty of sun block and a cap. If it's summer bring an umbrella—good for sun and rain—and your own food and beverages. If it's hot, you will want to bring plenty of water. Bring along a good length of sturdy chain in case you wind up having something follow you home.

## Nonprofit and Charity Auctions

Some nonprofit organizations, foundations, churches, and other charities hold auctions that will occasionally include collectible vehicles. The money from the sale is dedicated to a worthy cause. A small, struggling country church I have visited raises enough money to meet its entire annual heat bill with a well-planned weekend-long vintage car, truck, and motorcycle show that includes an auction on the last day.

Nestled in the hills along the St. Lawrence River, near Quebec City, the Domaine Museum is home to 35 exquisitely restored automobiles. The Domaine Foundation supports single mothers.

A shining example of a charitable auction is one sponsored annually by The Domaine Museum, a well-known classic and collectible automobile museum located near Quebec City, in the picturesque village of Pohénégamook. Folks come from Europe and all over North America to take part in this worthy event. Beautiful vehicles cross the auction block. The proceeds are earmarked for the museum's foundation, dedicated to bringing joy into the lives of the children of single mothers, kids who far too often go without life's very basics.

Jim Lenzke, the technical editor for this book, bought a 1977 Oldsmobile Delta 88 Royale at an auction held for the benefit of the Rawhide Boys Ranch in New London, Wisconsin. Troubled teens live here. They get a chance to straighten out their lives and learn to be good citizens. Every May, the institution puts on a collector car auction where 40 to 70 cars are sold. The proceeds from the sale go to support an establishment that exists on donations.

Founded in 1965 to give troubled teenaged boys a second chance at life, the Rawhide Boys Ranch (www.rawhide.org) has been auctioning off cars, jewelry, and other luxury goods since 1983. Celebrities like NFL Hall of Famer Bart Starr donate personal vehicles to the auction.

## Sealed-Bid Auctions

There is no drama associated with a sealed bid auction. Bidders simply write down the price they are willing to pay for the desired vehicle and deposit it with the secretary or clerk. On the appointed date the envelopes are opened, and the one containing the highest bid is notified.

Sealed-bid auctions can be long, drawn-out affairs, lasting a number of months. Before you place a bid, find out if it can be withdrawn, should your circumstances change.

The Chevrolet Corvair Monza Spyder offered four-on-the-floor and bucket seats. It prompted Ford to respond with the Mustang.

Most municipal, regional, and county governments have auctions as the need arises. There is no set time for these auctions; they usually take place when there is no more physical space to keep the vehicles!

My friends, Myron Leonard and his son Michael, placed a sealed bid at the Franklin County Courthouse for an auction that included a 1963 GMC fire truck. The truck had served the Village of Constable in New York's North Country for many years before being put to work flushing out culverts and washing bridges throughout Franklin County. To the Leonards' surprise, the $176.25 offered for the pumper turned out to be the highest bid. Now, father and son own a big, red, noisy 10,000-pound toy with only 17,000 miles on the odometer.

To increase your chances of being the highest bidder in a sealed bid auction, pencil in an odd figure; one slightly higher than what you know the commonly accepted value to be. If the going rate for that 1979 Plymouth Volare police cruiser is $2,000, a bid of $2,019.37 will give you an advantage over everyone who bids the flat two grand.

## Online Auctions

Many reputable houses hold virtual auctions, complete with online catalogs and online bidding. This is a fairly new phenomenon. The subject is vast and deserves to be examined in detail. Since the focus of this book is about real time auctions, the topic of online auctions will not be dealt with here. While there are many bargains to be had without leaving the comfort of your home, do be cautious. One can get a little too relaxed over a bottle of vintage French wine and, like one Michigan couple I know, wind up bidding on and owning a 1950 Packard they never intended to buy.

Online auctions are an easy way to get initiated into the auto auction world. The biggest drawback is that many of the deals fall apart. That has prompted more and more folks to turn to real auctions in order to satisfy their desire to participate.

Complaints to police about fraud resulting from Internet auctions have increased by more than 1000 percent since 1998.

Now that you have become acquainted with the more common types of auctions, you are ready to meet some of the folks who host these events. They vary widely and cater to a complete range of tastes and pocketbooks.

## Meet Some of the Players

Many of the auction firms have national and international reputations of the highest order. They are la crème-de-la-crème of the automotive auction world. A few of these esteemed houses are listed here in alphabetical order.

### The Barrett-Jackson Auction Company

www.barrett-jackson.com

Barrett-Jackson's first auction took place in 1971 in Scottsdale, Arizona. Its modest goal was to raise money for the local library. The event has grown throughout the years to include banquets for charities and gala evenings for invitees. In 2005, the auction brought in more than $60 million in sales at the annual January event, seen by millions on television. Every one of the 875 cars that crossed the auction block that year were sold at No Reserve, which means there is no minimum price required by the seller. More than 200,000 visitors registered and approximately $2 million was raised for charity work at the two gala events. The auction house also holds events in California and Florida.

Barrett-Jackson's facilities include a showroom where one can find cars for sale on consignment. One can also make arrangements to bring in a vehicle for evaluation.

### Bonhams & Butterfields

www.bonhams.com

This venerable British firm has more than two centuries of experience behind its auction belt. The highly esteemed auction house has reached across the Atlantic Ocean to offer first tier collectible automobile auction events in Brookline, Massachusetts; Greenwich, Connecticut; and Quail Lodge, California.

### Kruse International

www.kruseinternational.com

Located in Auburn, Indiana, Kruse held its first auction in 1971, as well. The "granddaddy of auction companies" was owned briefly by eBay but came back into the hands of the Kruse family in 2002. Today, more than 300,000 people flock to the weeklong Labor Day event in the Hoosier State. More than 5,000 automobiles crossed the auction block in 2004 and approximately 65 percent of them were sold. In addition to the Auburn event, the company holds approximately 30 auctions throughout the United States during the course of the year.

The Kruse Labor Day auction is part of the annual Auburn Cord Duesenberg Festival, a weeklong Hoosier tradition that marks its Golden Anniversary in 2006.

### Mecum Collector Car Auctioneers

www.mecumauction.com

Located in Marengo, Illinois, this firm holds auctions throughout the United States. They specialize in muscle cars and hot rods.

### RM Auctions, Inc.

www.rmauctions.com

This impeccable classic car restoration company has been around since 1979. In 1991, it expanded into the auction scene. Already, the firm has surpassed the $100 million mark in annual sales. RM Auctions holds between 10 and 12 auctions a year and is best known for its spring and fall classic car events in Toronto, its vintage motor cars event at Meadow Brook, Michigan, and the Sports & Classic Car Auction held each September in Monterey, California.

## Regional and Specialty Houses

There are many well-known, well-respected specialty houses throughout the United States and Canada that handle sales of collectible vehicles in an auction setting. Space does not permit a complete list of regional auctioneers, but firms with solid reputations include the Kensington

Motor Group in New York State (www.hamptonautoclassic.com). Silver Auctions, located in Washington State, produces 30 auctions a year in 10 western states and Canada (www.silverauctions.com). Their annual Hot August Nights extravaganza in Reno, Nevada, is widely recognized as one of the season's premier collector car events. MidAmerica Auctions (www.midamericaauctions.com) in Roseville, Minnesota, is another regional player as is Cox Auctions (www.bransonauction.com) in Branson, Missouri. If pristine automobiles aren't your thing the vintage junkyard VanDerBrink auction (www.vanderbrinkauctions.com) held in Garrison, South Dakota, may very well turn your crank!

### Meet Jim Cox — Cox Auctions

Jim Cox has owned Cox Auctions based in Branson, Missouri, since 1989. Jim was born in Fort Dodge, Iowa, and attended grade school there. When the family moved, the rest of his school years were spent in Bucks County, Pennsylvania, and Kansas City, Missouri, where he finished high school. From there, he went on to the Kansas City Art Institute and Kansas University in Lawrence where he studied fine arts. He married briefly and had a wonderful son, Ken. Jim's ambition to be the world's greatest painter was irrevocably altered when he discovered he was a good painter but even better at the business end of the craft. He opened an art gallery when he was 20.

*This 1952 Packard Mayfair Convertible was bought for $22,000, a bargain.*

Jim's budding art gallery career was interrupted when he was called to serve Uncle Sam from 1964 to 1967. Jim spent most of his time in Europe. He didn't meet any East German spies, but he had Top Secret security clearance, and his assignments were always interesting.

After mustering out of the service, Jim worked briefly in radio and newspaper advertising. He learned enough to know he wanted an agency of his own. In the meantime, he had met a girl in Paris who was from Oregon. They married and had two sons, Brian and Brandon. The family was born and raised in Oregon, and Jim went into the advertising agency business where he dealt primarily with new car dealers in Washington, Oregon, and northern California.

His full-service retail agency delivered everything from budgets to marketing to production for newspapers, magazines, radio, outdoor advertising, and television. Jim laughs as he recalls, "If you put on a big promotion and they did great, it was because they were good salesmen. If it fell flat, it was because of poor advertising." The learning curve was fast and Jim liked that.

Mark Trimble started the auction, Jim continues.

Jim has always loved cars, and one of his first memories is of his uncle's 1952 XK-120 Jaguar. The first car he owned was a 1932 Ford that he bought when he was 14. He spent his high school years turning the five-window coupe into a hot rod. The finished car sported a Chrysler Hemi complete with the pushbutton Torque-Flyte transmission. When he drove his creation to school, all the other guys were driving British, Italian, and German sports cars or Corvettes and Thunderbirds. Jim promptly gave up the deuce coupe for something more acceptable. Setting trends rather than following came later.

Years later in Oregon, a friend who knew Jim restored and raced cars told him he should go to a collector car auction to pick up a Mercedes. He went to Stu McCloud's auction in Seattle, and he wound up buying a 1974 Mercedes 450 SL for $12,000. The first time auction-goer was pleased with the bargain and remembers the sale and the car fondly. "You always make your profit when you buy," he says.

*This 1964 Austin-Healy sold for $39,500 in 2005.*

During the years he owned an ad agency, Jim was also producing the *Concours d'Elegance* at the Village Green in Cottage Grove, Oregon. During the 19 years he did that, he met a lot of collectors and developed his affinity for the people who owned the cars. "The cars are fantastic, full of history, and like pieces of mechanical fine art, but the real treasures are the people that own them," he points out. "It's the people I enjoy most."

Jim moved back to Branson, Missouri, in 1988 to help take care of his parents who had retired to the area in the 1960s. He met Kathy Boyle through old friends on a visit to Kansas City, and they fell in love. Judge Hough was a good friend and a car collector, and one day he asked Jim and Kathy when they were going to get married. Jim said, "Oh, one day when you've got time." Judge Hough made time real quick, and the couple was married.

Having cared for his parents, Jim was ready to pack up and leave Branson when Mark Trimble, one of Branson's founding fathers, had a chat with him. Mark was a big car collector and had established a car museum. He didn't enjoy the museum anymore and, with Dean Kruse, began the liquidation of the 300+ car collection. After the collection was gone, it became a consignment auction. Mark tired of that quickly but knew it was a viable event and good for the community.

*No reserve. I wonder why?*

Mark made Jim an offer he couldn't refuse, and suddenly he owned an auction. It was 1989 and the bottom of the market. Despite the poor market conditions, 300 cars were consigned. He lost between $50,000 and $35,000 each year until his first profit in 1991. Jim had faith in the auction and kept it going because he knew the value of the market. It did bounce back eventually and remains successful to this day. Jim doesn't forget charities, either. He has two favorites, the Salvation Army and Big Brothers/Big Sisters, both of which do good work.

The attendance at the April and October events runs between 3,000 and 7,000 people. They come from the Midwestern states and as far away as California, Florida, New England, Ireland, Norway, and New Zealand. That is phenomenal for a stand-alone event, but in Branson, there is always plenty to do. There are a good dozen family-oriented resorts with headline acts. Branson may have only 6,800 residents, but the town plays host to 7 million visitors a year and boasts 44,000 theatre seats and 25,000 hotel rooms. Jim makes sure that his auctions end at six o'clock so folks can paint the town.

In 16 years, Jim has watched sales grow from $300,000 to more than $4 million per sale. Chevrolets, Fords, MoPars, and classics dominate on the block, but Jim notes that sports cars are beginning to have an impact.

*Jim and shop foreman, Bruce, unload a 1931 Phaeton.*

The auction business is fun, but Jim bought the Candlestick Inn restaurant in 1995. Located on Mt. Branson overlooking the downtown, the place is charming. Jim liked the fine food and the casual atmosphere. One evening he was eating dinner and heard it was for sale. The next day he and a car-collecting friend owned it. Jim loves traditions, and the Candlestick Inn, like Branson itself, suits him perfectly. Steak, seafood, roast duck, and quail are prepared by some of the nation's finest chefs.

Jim and Kathy collect old cars and mahogany boats. They like to use them on Table Rock Lake with its 840 miles of shoreline. They have a cat named Cricket, and Dozer, supposedly his son's dog, is a Bull Mastiff. The pets don't get to go boating, but they both like to ride in the cars.

*This 1941 Buick sold in 2004 for $54,000.*

Jim has been buying at auctions for 30 years and owned an auction house for 15 years. He knows that the biggest mistake that buyers make is not doing the necessary research. He gives a good example of due diligence. A gentleman brought in a 1966 Ford Mustang Shelby GT 350 H. These were rent-a-racers from Hertz. Jim Wicks of the Shelby Club was asked to assess the authenticity of the vehicle and came back with the bad news that it had been re-bodied. The owner was promptly notified as was a client who had come to bid on the car. A public announcement was made that the car was a re-body. The value dropped. The owner had hoped for $85,000 to $90,000 but under the circumstances accepted a high bid of $72,000. Several days later, the new owner suffered an attack of buyer's remorse and wanted his money back because it was a re-body. The house refused because he had been duly advised as to the car's state before the auction, and it had been publicly announced as well. If that wasn't sufficient, the three video cameras that capture the entire event recorded the transaction. Fortunately for the buyer, an intelligent, sophisticated, and longtime collector, he was able to sell the car, with full disclosure, and to make a small profit.

*This is a beautiful re-body on a Ford Model T.*

According to Jim, the second biggest mistake is not understanding how helpful the ringman is. A new bidder needs to establish a rapport with the ringman who is there to straighten out any confusion, keep bidders on track, and tell them where the current bid stands. The ringman is there to help the buyers get what they want. Jim always knows what he wants to buy, and he always goes to the same ringman when possible. At Barrett-Jackson, he always tells ringman Tim Assiter to count him in up to a certain limit. No one knows he is bidding and only if his limit is exceeded will Tim turn to Jim and ask, "Do you want to continue?" This eliminates confusion, keeps him under his limit, and allows him to stay anonymous. When a known collector is bidding on a car, it is not unheard of for a friend of the seller to advance the bid. This is wrong, but it happens. If a known collector is anonymous, there is less chance of the seller's advances.

*This 1956 Eldo Biaritz brought in $69,900.*

Another key for Jim is that bidders need to understand the rules for cars being offered with a reserve. "With Reserve" means that the seller will not accept less than a certain amount. Because of that, the auctioneer has the right and responsibility to advance the bid to or near the reserve amount. This not only saves time but keeps the bidding realistic as well. Why keep asking for a bid of $20,000 when it will take close to $40,000 to buy the car? It's a reality that is often misunderstood.

Registering is also something that Jim encourages auction-goers to do. Many potential buyers, usually first-timers, will attend an auction without having registered to bid. It's a common

*Ready for presale inspection.*

mistake but often misunderstood, especially by people with considerable resources. They cannot understand why they should have to disclose personal information, especially about their finances. It's quite simple really. Would you accept a check from someone you didn't know who wants to leave your driveway with your car and your title? The auction company spends a great deal of time verifying a bidder's funds. That service alone is worth the entry fee from sellers who expect to be paid after the hammer drops.

Jim also points out that one of the biggest and most repeated mistakes of sellers is waiting until the last minute to register their car for a particular sale. By doing so they miss out on all the publicity and advertising paid for by the auction company. The strategy should be to select a company that is established, has a large advertising budget, and has a tradition of "high percentage" sales. The seller should take advantage of these benefits by registering his or her car early, providing as much documentation as possible as well as high quality photography that can be easily reproduced. The more information the auction company has about a particular car, the more they can provide potential buyers. Good auction companies spend endless hours prior to each sale contacting buyers who are interested in specific cars. The seller of a collector car has invested thousands of dollars and probably hundreds of hours preparing it for a potential sale. Why stop short when selling by not taking advantage of everything a good auction company can do for you?

*Jim bought this 1948 MG TC in Oklahoma for $14,000. Five years later it sold for $24,500.*

The question most often asked of Jim by someone wanting to start into the collector car hobby is, "What should I buy?" Jim's answer is simple and obvious, "Only buy what you really like." "But I hear muscle cars are doing really well," the person says. "Yes, they are. Is there one in particular that you really like?" Jim then asks. "Well, no, I just heard that they're a really good investment," the person responds. "Are you looking for an investment or a collector car?" Jim queries.

Okay, you can see where that one is going, so let's try this. Jim bought some Sirius Satellite Radio stock at $7.50 a share. It went down to $6 and is currently up to $7.11. Was that a good investment? Not yet. He once bought a 1964 Thunderbird convertible for $11,500. When he got it home and discovered its needs, Jim proceeded to spend about $6,000 on the car. At the time that he bought it, the high end for that car was about $15,000. It took two years for the prices to come up to equal the investment. Jim then sold the car and broke even.

*This 1948 International sold in 2002 for $22,000. Its worth increased to about $50,000 by 2006.*

What's the difference between Sirius Satellite Radio stock and a classic car? Well, Jim says he has never driven a stock certificate around the block. He has never had anyone (except his broker) say, "That's a nice stock you got there." Jim says he's never shared the history of Sirius Satellite Radio with a 14-year-old who didn't know that Ford once manufactured cars with disappearing tops and over 400-cubic-inch motors and made the little girl down the street get big eyes when the car went past her.

So, buy what you really like, even if it's a '52 Nash Rambler Convertible! If that's what you like—it conjures up good memories and *you* think it's fun—then do it. It's a hobby. Enjoy the memories, admire the design and engineering, preserve the history, and share it with anyone who will listen, especially kids!

Jim Cox's five rules for collecting cars:

1. Have a safe place to keep them.
2. Only spend what you can really afford.
3. Do your research before you buy.
4. Make it better than when you bought it.
5. Share it with people who care.

Jim Cox's five rules for which cars to collect:

1. Only buy what you really like.
2. Remember the food chain: Convertibles first, horsepower second, and styling always.
3. Rare doesn't mean desirable.
4. Like location with real estate, remember condition, condition, condition.
5. A good history is better than a new fad.

# 7 AUCTION FEVER

## DISPELLING MYTHS ABOUT AUCTIONS

### You Will Buy a Vehicle You Don't Want and Didn't Bid On

One of the most widespread myths in the world of auctions is that an inadvertent movement of the hand or head will get the auctioneer's nod as a bid. As a result, you are likely to wind up with a vehicle you never intended to bid on.

There was a time when folks did wink an eye, tip a hat, scratch their noses, or tug on their ears to indicate a discrete bid. My dad's favorite was to hook his thumbs in his overalls then stick out two fingers to indicate he was bidding. Secret signals are about as common as top hats and spats these days. The auctioneer and the bidder assistants sweep the audience looking for cards or paddles held high. If you wave at your spouse who happens to be on the other side of the arena to get her to bring you a coffee and your waving gesture is mistaken for a bid, or you do bid in error, speak up immediately and the situation will be corrected. Likewise, if the auctioneer thinks you have bid, you will be asked. Nobody wants you to buy a vehicle you didn't actually bid on!

Tommy, a.k.a. "Spanky," Assiter is the industry's best-known auctioneer. As a veteran in the business, he has seen it all. Bidders who wish to be discrete or even remain anonymous occasionally approach Spanky before a sale to arrange a secret system with him. For those few who do use secret signals, the cigar-in-the-mouth bid or the crossed-arm bid are common. Spanky tells the amusing story of a man who once bid using the crossed-arm method. When the price got too high, the man shot his arms out wide like an airplane to indicate he had dropped out. His anonymity was blown, but he made darned sure he wasn't in the fray anymore. The incident still makes Spanky chuckle.

He also recalls a famous person who didn't want anyone present to know he was bidding. The celebrity met with the auctioneer before the sale and told him, "As long as I have my pen out of my pocket, I'm bidding." Spanky agreed to keep an eye out for the pen. During the bidding, the gentleman was interrupted by a fan who asked for his autograph. Spanky watched as the man signed his name and then absentmindedly put the pen in his pocket. The pre-arranged signal had been that the man was out of the bidding when he put away the pen. Spanky didn't know why the man had put the pen away, but he was sure the man had dropped out. Suddenly it dawned on the man that Spanky was no longer paying attention to him, and he franticly scrambled to find that pen. The hammer went down, and he lost out on his vehicle as he fumbled around in his pocket.

If you make a secret signal arrangement with the auctioneer or a ringman, be sure to remember it and use it consistently throughout the auction!

## The Highest Bid Is the Final Price

This is not always the case for several reasons. First, if the vehicle carried a reserve price and that price was not met while it was on the block, it will be returned to the corral. The vehicle may be run through again, returned to the owner, or sold to an individual after the block as a result of negotiations orchestrated by an auction house staff member between the owner and a prospective buyer.

On rare occasions the highest bidder is unable to take delivery of the vehicle. The auction staff keeps careful track of the other bidders and will offer the car to those bidders left at the end when the hammer dropped, should that ever happen.

## Only Vehicles with Problems Sell at Auctions

There are many reasons for an owner to sell a vehicle at an auction. Dumping a problem car is generally not one of them. Now, that was not always the case. Several decades ago there were far more collectors than there were vehicles. The same tired, high mileage cars could be seen crossing the auction block time and time again. Automotive historian and auction critic Matt Joseph recalls a time when "dogs" changed owners so frequently they could "find their way home without an owner." More than one auctioneer was heard to quip in half jest, "This car gets to more auctions than I do." Today there are plenty of quality vehicles to go around.

The car on the block may not have any problems at all, but it is important to remember that vehicles sold at auctions are there for a reason. A quality car will enjoy a highly desirable reputation. Folks know the owner and the vehicle. Often, the choicest and most collectible wheels in the world are traded privately among friends and only ever see the auction block when a collection is liquidated at an estate sale.

Savvy Tip

Common reasons for a car seeing the auctioneer's block these days are because of death, illness, divorce, personal economic downturn, or lifestyle downsizing. There are a growing number of folks who buy and restore a collector car then place it in an auction so that the pleasurable process can be repeated.

## Auction Houses Set Collector Vehicle Prices

That auction houses set the value of collectible vehicles is a myth, well at least partially. The large houses are certainly part of the mix when it comes to establishing values, but other factors weigh in heavily, too. There are men like the legendary Ken Buttolph, who was the longtime editor of the six-tier price guide for *The Standard Catalog of Cars & Prices*. He eats

The 1980 Concord from American Motors was a posh very upscale compact. It has not yet caught on with collectors.

and sleeps vintage vehicles every day of the year and travels throughout the country to observe them as they change hands. These vehicles may be auctions, private sales, estate sales, and trades. Buttolph talks to key collectors on a regular basis. He tracks the sale history of vehicles throughout decades. Using this information, he evaluates the price ceiling one should pay for any particular model.

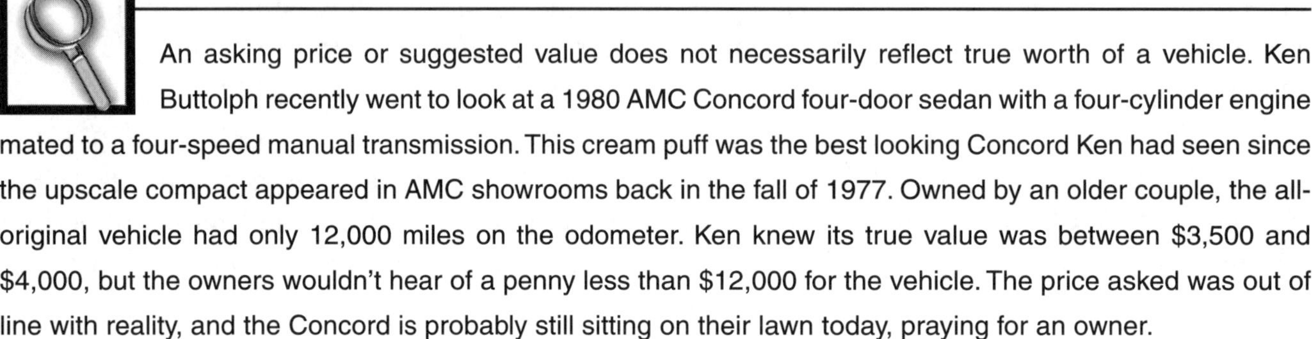

An asking price or suggested value does not necessarily reflect true worth of a vehicle. Ken Buttolph recently went to look at a 1980 AMC Concord four-door sedan with a four-cylinder engine mated to a four-speed manual transmission. This cream puff was the best looking Concord Ken had seen since the upscale compact appeared in AMC showrooms back in the fall of 1977. Owned by an older couple, the all-original vehicle had only 12,000 miles on the odometer. Ken knew its true value was between $3,500 and $4,000, but the owners wouldn't hear of a penny less than $12,000 for the vehicle. The price asked was out of line with reality, and the Concord is probably still sitting on their lawn today, praying for an owner.

## Auctioneers Can't Be Understood

Auctioneers are trained professionals. They sell goods using a special patter they developed while in school. That sales patter is unique, informative, and meant to be entertaining as well, so listen carefully until you get used to it. Auctioneers speak fast to keep the flow of goods moving quickly. If you just flew in to attend an auction in Biloxi, Mississippi, from Presque Isle, Maine, your ears will need more than a few minutes to become acclimatized to the different accent, colloquial expressions, and speech patterns, too.

The auctioneer's cry or chant is made up of three parts: the first part is the amount of money that has been bid, then some information is added, and that leads up to the third part of the chant, the amount of new bid being asked for by the auctioneer. If you're having trouble following along, concentrate on the numbers and don't get caught up in the patter. If an auctioneer is speaking so quickly that the audience can't understand, then he or she is not doing the job properly.

Don't be embarrassed to stop the show and ask questions if you don't understand what is being said. The auctioneer is there to sell items and wants to be sure that everyone hears and understands clearly.

## The Auctioneer Speaks the Gospel Truth

The auctioneer doesn't lie but do remember that the information he or she has about the vehicle on the block was supplied by the seller. It is impossible for the house staff to verify every fact about every vehicle that will go on the block. They do their very best to weed out any fake and fraudulent vehicles that might appear. Auctioneers use plenty of hype in selling, and as they reel off the facts, they are careful to say "so says the owner" and "according to the owner."

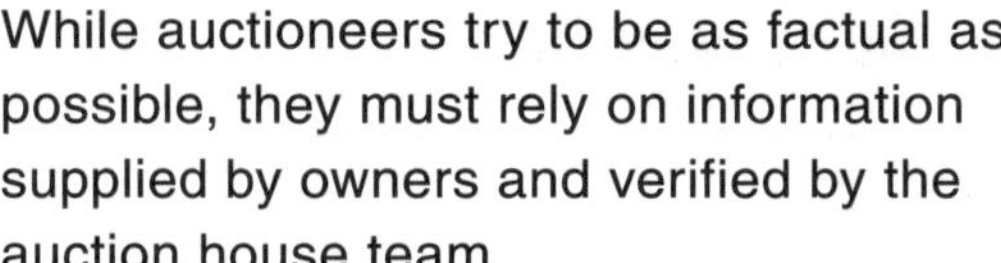

While auctioneers try to be as factual as possible, they must rely on information supplied by owners and verified by the auction house team.

## Everything at an Auction Is a Bargain

While the vast majority of auction houses are scrupulously honest and there are bargains to be had, not every vehicle is going to be in the condition you think it is. It is possible to lose on what initially appeared to be an incredible deal. Only careful examination of the vehicle will prevent disappointment with a purchase.

If it seems too good to be true, it probably is!

# Common Pitfalls to Avoid

## The Bar

Many of the bigger events feature an open bar. Wetting one's whistle can be a mixed blessing. Knocking back a fine single malt scotch or a smart drink with a little umbrella in it adds to the festive atmosphere, and the vast majority of folks in attendance hold their liquor well. There are those few who may have one too many. It can happen on occasion that folks drink too much. Fueled with liquid courage they may bid far in excess of reality. They may even become verbally abusive or physically belligerent. When they cross the line, security guards will remove them from the auction.

If you choose to drink alcohol at an auction, the guideline is to drink with the same moderation that you would if you were going to get behind the wheel of a vehicle.

While most bidders are not willing to go beyond the auctioneers' predictions, or even the estimated current value of an object, bidding can soar wildly above the current prices and suggested guidelines fly right out the window. Buying a vehicle in front of an audience heightens emotions considerably. The desire to be a victorious winner or, equally, the fear of being seen as a losing bidder can awaken a near ferocious state of primitive competition. Suddenly, in the fast-paced auction setting, the normally mild-mannered pastor must win at all costs.

## Stupid Money

Millions watched on television as a 1969 Camaro Z-28, 302 V-8 with dual four-barrel cross ram induction—a dealer-installed option that the factory wouldn't put in the car—rolled onto the block at Barrett-Jackson a couple of seasons ago. The yellow car with its black rally stripes and hood gaps was an obvious hurry-up job. One reporter figured it would hit $50,000, tops. Bidding opened at $40,000 and skyrocketed to $80,000 in under a minute. It was obvious that the car matched the man's blazer and that appeared to be the sole factor driving the wild bidding. The muscle car entered rarified territory, even for a Camaro. The ringmen were waving their arms in the air getting the crowd to cheer, and the auctioneers revved up for what is known in auction circles as "stupid money." The hammer came down on the fast bowtie at $120,000.

The Camaro was Chevrolet's response to the Ford Mustang in the battle for the pony car market.

The Camaro was Chevrolet's entry into the pony car game. Arriving for the 1967 season, it bowed along with its cousin, the Pontiac Firebird. The pair from GM joined the Plymouth Barracuda, the AMC Marlin, the Ford Mustang, and its stable mate, the Mercury Cougar.

Longtime auctioneer Spanky Assiter has a little different view on the matter of stupid money. It is his astute observation that there is no such thing as stupid money. He recalls using those very words to describe the situation when Tom Monaghan, owner of the Domino's Pizza chain, dropped $1.5 million on a 1931 Bugatti Royale at an auction. The story was news and appeared in countless newspapers. The deal generated a lot of publicity for business. Within a short period of time, the pizza king was offered $11.5 million for the same vehicle. He parted with the car and pocketed a lot of dough. If the initial event was newsworthy, that second story was absolutely sensational and hit virtually every newspaper in North America. The publicity did wonders for pizza sales. Spanky marvelled at the deal and how it played out. He promptly retracted every comment he ever made about "stupid money."

## Auction Fever

The entire overbidding phenomenon has been identified as "auction fever." The final cost will be driven by how valuable the car is to the bidder, who will single-handedly redefine the worth of that vehicle in the economy. In order to bid sanely, a bidder must be calm, cool, and collected. The worst thing that can happen is to get angry, lose control, and run up the price of a vehicle far beyond its accepted value. A well-rehearsed strategy firmly fixed in your mind will help you stick to a plan.

## Winner's Curse

Often the price of a vehicle is driven far higher than the current market value because one or more bidders have not done the requisite homework. Bidding on a vehicle at an auction, armed with erroneous or incomplete information and a strong gut feeling, each wave of the paddle drives the price farther from true market value. A successful bidder who has overpaid substantially for the prize on the block is said to have the "winner's curse."

Exercise caution and use common sense when bidding. Winning isn't everything.

## Self-Justification

Another sociological phenomenon exhibited at auctions is a self-justification of actions, sometimes called the "escalation of commitment." Here, the bidders know exactly what the vehicle is worth because the homework has been done. Since considerable time and effort have been invested, these bidders somehow feel that the vehicle on the floor must be theirs, no matter what the cost. Any pre-determined limits are thrown out the window, along with any common sense. This becomes an out-and-out competition, one that must result in victory, no matter if bidding hits the stratosphere. These bidders cannot justify having invested all the time, money, effort, absence from work, and travel costs they have sunk into the project unless they actually go home with the vehicle they came for in the first place.

## Competitive Arousal

Another commonly observed behavior is that of competition, a.k.a. "competitive arousal." Ownership of the vehicle becomes secondary to the overwhelming need to eliminate all competitors. These bidders are susceptible to the "win at all costs" syndrome for any number or combination of pressures including rivalry, awareness of being watched by the audience, time constraint, even the pressure to look good at an event because of heavy pre-auction advertising. In the mind of the bidder, the other bidders are far more than competitors; they have become adversaries, enemies of the highest order.

An astute auctioneer will note competitive arousal characteristics in various individuals in the crowd and play up to them by using carefully chosen language designed to deepen the need to win. After all, the auctioneer is present on behalf of the seller.

## Practice Does Not Make Perfect

Research has shown that there is no drop in the frequency of these kinds of behaviors in patrons who attend auctions regularly compared to those who attend auction events only occasionally. People who are high strung, easily excitable, are overly sensitive to what they perceive others think about them, or take things personally are all prime candidates to overbid at an auction. Further studies will no doubt be conducted to determine more underlying causes in this fascinating field.

Auctions are just plain fun. They are a welcome diversion to our everyday lives and provide an opportunity to slip away from the daily grind. When not personally involved, the intense bidding wars offer first class entertainment. Each item on the block unfolds into a drama for those in attendance. This is good, clean fun, an event to which one can bring the entire family. In a day and age when fewer and fewer people go on outings, it is comforting to know that an auction is wholesome enough for the family to enjoy together.

Some studies show that overbidding happens more frequently and by higher amounts at a live auction than an online auction. On the other hand, The Commonwealth of Massachusetts operates both types of auctions and notes that an item sold online will frequently fetch as much as twice the price of an item sold at a live auction.

# 8 PROS AND CONS OF AUCTION BUYING

## Reasons for Buying at an Auction

In the sophisticated, high-tech twenty-first century, occasions for humans to go hunting are extremely limited. We have tamed just about everything there is. The vast majority of folks who attend auctions quickly discover a genuine thrill runs through the very core of their beings as they stake out and bid on their dream cars. Somehow, an auction awakens and sharpens latent, primal hunting instincts, instincts as old as the human race.

There is no way to rank the advantages of auction buying in any order; that is simply too subjective a task. However, it is certainly true that the auction experience is a deeply satisfying one on many levels.

Attending a live auction is genuine entertainment, an event that simply can't be duplicated in front of a television set or a computer. The action at a live auction event is always unpredictable; the element of surprise hangs heavily in the air.

Auctions bring people together in a light-hearted, festive atmosphere. It is commerce turned into a social affair. There is no substitute for the real time rubbing of shoulders with like-minded buyers, meeting and greeting friends, chatting, broadening your knowledge of vintage vehicles, and sharpening your buying skills. Many folks form lifelong friendships at auctions.

The National Auctioneers Association commissioned two very comprehensive studies in 2003. It was determined that the number one reason people take in auctions is not for the buying or selling that takes place, not even for the hope of purchasing something at bargain basement prices. No, the primary reason for attending was the excitement an auction generates. An astonishing 100 percent of the people surveyed were of the opinion that auctions were fun. Surprisingly, the majority of those surveyed indicated they travel as far as 90 minutes to attend a good auction.

Because a vintage car auction is held on a specific date, lasts only for a short, fixed period of time, it is easy to recognize it as a special occasion. An auction date will be marked on the calendar and given much more importance than a conventional sale. You don't think so? I know lots of homes where a favorite annual auction event is already penciled into the agenda book—for next year. I don't know of anyone who has ever circled a date on the calendar and made an appointment to drive down to a local car dealer for the purpose of checking out the wheels on the lot.

Other studies have shown that any kind of buying is an emotional experience. We are moved each time we make a purchase because the object sought is something we need or desire. That holds true whether it is a Torino Talladega or a tube of toothpaste that is under consideration. Because we always want the highest quality at the lowest price, we are driven to shop.

A profile of the average buyer at one of the major antique automobile auction events reveals that 90 percent are male and that the average age is 50. Most are self-made men or CEOs of major companies. These men include successful farmers, construction kings, software moguls, and inventors. They do not buy for investment purposes; they are on hand to shop for toys. Women make up an ever-growing segment of the market; many experts feel that the rise of women bidders is the direct result of auctions being televised.

As we look around at the cars on display at the auction, many fond memories will wash over us. Once I attended an auction with my dad, who had his heart set on taking home a 1923 Nash. Dad was a seasoned auction-goer, an old pro who knew all the old-time signals and could read an audience with the same ease as he could predict the weather from looking at the sky or calculate the temperature by listening to crickets chirp. He knew every trick in the auctioneer's book. A fixture at auctions, Dad was well known for his faded overalls and railroad cap. He

Competing in the upper luxury class was this lovely 1923 Nash Model 47. The closed sedan listed for $1,445.

always had a ready smile, a handshake, always told a good joke followed by his trademark conspiratorial wink.

Completely out of character, dad doggedly bid on that Nash until it was his. The hammer price was a good $800 over the suggested value. You can bet I was dying of curiosity and could hardly wait to hear this story. I was willing to bet a whole maple sugar pie that he was privy to some long-lost secret, something intriguing like the Nash once belonged to a rum runner and the undersides of the horsehair seats were stuffed with $100 bills.

Over a meatloaf and mashed potato dinner at the Blue Bird Diner, I finally coaxed the story out of him. "When I was six," he said, between bites, "I was walking from the farm into town. Doc Albertson pulled up in his big blue Nash and asked me if I'd like a ride. Why, I was thrilled to death. I had never ridden in a motorcar before. I thought I had died and gone to heaven, sitting on that leather seat like a prince. I fell in love with Nash that day and vowed when I grew up I'd own a Nash of my own. I've never owned any other kind of car until they switched to Ramblers and I bought those, too. That's Doc Albertson's car that I bought," he confided. "It is the very same car I took my first ride in. Now, young man," he said, with a wink, "don't you dare breathe a word to your mother about what I paid for it. She'll holler for a new fridge."

Dad has gone to his rest, but at every auction I attend, I half expect to see him standing nearby, that crooked little grin on his face, thumbs hooked in those faded overalls, running up a bid just a tad, to irk a neighbor.

Another reason to buy at an auction is because it is a highly efficient process. There is no physical shopping, no running from one place to the next in hopes of finding what you want. The auction people have located your dream wheels and brought them to you physically, in the auction catalog or online. You most likely found your prize while sitting in a comfy chair and sipping a triple espresso or a double scotch. In fact, by viewing a wide range of vehicles presented in the catalog, or online, your horizons are actually broadened considerably. You already know if you aren't successful in obtaining vehicle "A," you know that you would be perfectly content with vehicle "B," and vehicle "C" would look just as sweet with you behind the wheel.

You are already pumped, primed, and motivated to make the purchase. You know that you will buy the vehicle, if the price is right. Having done your homework thoroughly, there will be no surprises. An adorable 1951 Henry J that you never knew you wanted and now simply must own, no matter what the price, won't pop up to surprise you and empty your wallet while your previously prized dream car slips through your fingers.

Stylists gave the 1966 Ford Falcon very pleasing lines. The little compact is often undervalued at auctions today.

## The Bidder Is in Control of the Purchase Process

Bidders set the price and subsequently the value of every vehicle that crosses the block. The very premise of the auction is based on variable pricing, that is, there is no fixed value for any item offered. Bid well, bargain hard, but be prudent!

A unique aspect of auctions is that you, the consumer, sit in the driver's seat. This is the only time this ever happens in the world of commerce. Registered bidders are in that unique position of power because, with each raise of the paddle, they control the determined value of the vehicle glittering on the auction block. The seller does not—and cannot—negotiate its worth. The seller is completely removed from the auction process.

I know a man who wanted a 1959 Edsel so bad he could taste it. Folks down the road had one sitting in their barn but weren't willing to sell it. He would check with them every spring and fall to see if they were willing to sell. On occasion, the owner would give a price but raise it at the last minute. This went on for more than 20 years. It was only after the owner died that his widow was willing to strike a deal, just to empty out the barn.

The Ford Motor Company did not offer a full range of automobiles in its stable like General Motors or Chrysler. GM offered the entry-priced Chevrolet, then one moved up to Pontiac, then on to Oldsmobile, and upward again to Buick before finally reaching the top of the corporate ladder with the purchase of a luxurious Cadillac. Chrysler Corporation matched GM's offerings with Plymouth, Dodge, DeSoto, Chrysler, and the sumptuous Imperial. Dearborn had a vast gap between its low-priced Ford and the majestic Lincoln. The upper mid-priced Mercury line was added in 1939 but didn't complete the lock-step range. To that end, the Edsel was introduced in the fall of 1957. It was the wrong product at the wrong time. The mid-priced market was disappearing as consumers opted for smaller cars. Edsel lasted only three model years before it was canned.

At an auction, there is no waiting or haggling of any kind. Traditional bargaining can take days, weeks, months, even years! All that dancing and dickering is eliminated at an auction. Time limits are fixed: the selling process is accelerated and compacted into a miniscule time frame. Sellers are highly motivated to accept the gavel price because they know the actual date they will receive their money for the transaction.

Bidders hold the ultimate say. The auctioneer will continue to accept bids until personal price limits have been surpassed and bidders drop out. You will never pay one red cent more than you think the vehicle is worth if you are well disciplined and stick to your limits. Don't get carried away! Even if you are the highest bidder and the hammer price is higher than the suggested guideline, you can take satisfaction in knowing that you have set a new benchmark for the value of that particular make and model of vehicle.

Unless the reserve has not been met, those dream wheels will be yours if you are the last one to raise your paddle!

The 1970 Dodge Dart could be had with the 340 V-8 engine and a fully synchronized three-speed transmission. The MoPar compact was hot when new and still sizzles today.

Another beauty of auctions is that the entire process is a transparent one. You have ample opportunity to view the merchandise, evaluate its worth to you, then make an informed decision before bidding in the open atmosphere provided by the auction venue.

Auctions are an equal opportunity sale experience. Totally democratic in nature, there are no favorites; choice vehicles are never squirreled away for preferred buyers. Your chances of going home with your dream wheels are every bit as good of those as the folks against whom you bid, as long as you have the boldest nerve and the deepest pockets.

There are plenty of deals to be had at auctions with the not so perfect examples that cross the block. This is especially true if you are handy with tools and willing to make some or all of the repairs and undertake the restoration required. While it doesn't happen every time, a savvy bidder with a wide range of restoration skills can often walk away from an auction with some terrific bargains.

An auction is a great way to start or add to a collection. Like the old Lay's potato chip advertisement—" bet you can't eat just one"— most collectors are seldom happy with just one vehicle. Soon there will be a second and a third. Then there are those all-important parts cars. Several years ago, a survey of a national American Motors club was conducted and yielded up the fact that the average number of cars per member was 12. Of the dozen, 10 were parts cars.

The 1952 Kaiser Manhattan is of only modest interest with collectors today but it is guaranteed to turn heads at car shows.

## There Are Bargains to Be Had

Extraordinary deals are often found in ordinary "Mom and Pop" cars. Good examples of these everyday highway heroes include the Dodge Dart, Plymouth Valiant, Ford Falcon, Chevrolet Nova, and the second generation of Chevrolet Corvair with its unique engineering and timeless styling. Let us not forget Kaiser, Studebaker, Nash, Hudson, Rambler, and later AMC passenger cars. They all fit this bill, too.

Really nice cars sometimes go for a song. Ken Buttolph remembers a sharp 1975 Pontiac Grand Ville convertible that was parked far away from the stage, next to a fence at a big auction event. Few people in attendance wandered out that far and almost no one saw the car. When the righteous ragtop arrived on stage, it caught people off guard. The man who snapped it up bought it for next to nothing, flipped it later that day and pocketed a cool $10,000 in the process.

When you arrive at the auction site, be sure to look everywhere! Vehicles are sometimes parked in obscure places. Check behind those trailers, you might discover a chrome and steel dream.

## Reasons Not to Buy at an Auction

### An Auction Is a Show

An auction is a high-pressure, public venue where spectators look on as bidders vie for the car on the block. The pacing is lockstep, and this can be a nerve-wracking disadvantage for some. An auction might not be the place for you if you're not used to taking part in a show. If you need a boost to get started, some of the bigger auctions provide an open bar to those who hold bid cards. Beware, liquid courage can spell disaster!

### Addiction

Auctions can represent high stakes and as such can be addictive. They can be dangerous to people who have addictive personalities. The thrill of bidding over and over is replaced with temporary letdown, even sadness, once the item is owned, but the bidding can be repeated endlessly at auctions, sometimes with disastrous results.

Bob Nickels (not his real name) lives near Detroit. He is addicted to auctions. He says, "I have gone to an antique car auction and bought as many as four cars at the same sale. I didn't want them; I didn't need them. I just bought them because I could. I go home depressed. I take them back to the auction and sell them within three months, once the thrill of owning it wears off. I always lose money." Nickels' case is not unique. "I go to the auction with no intention of bidding," he explains. "I'm addicted. The minute I know there's going to be an auction, I'll try to get there. The overwhelming availability of all that chrome gets my blood going. You're away from home in a carnival atmosphere. As soon as I hear the auctioneer's patter, I'm right in there bidding against the competition. It's hypnotic. It's a hunt, a game, a contest. I have to do it." Nickels admits to losing more than $100,000 in the past four years. He looks sad for a moment then a twinkle comes into his eye as he says, "It doesn't even have to be a car auction. The energy levels are so high. It's pure excitement." He jokes, "Heck, I bought my wife at an auction."

The more highly advertised the auction, the more constrained the time limit for purchase at the end of the event, and the more visible bidders are to competitors and to the audience, the more likely there will be pressure on certain individuals who will respond by overbidding.

## Lack of Information

If you have not prepared properly, you may find yourself in trouble. Every one of the auction houses urges bidders to do their homework and to exercise "due diligence." Without knowledge it is highly likely that you will not have all the information you need to know if the vehicle you are bidding on is everything it is purported to be. If the car has not passed your personal inspection, let it go. There is no point in buying a "pig in a poke," especially if turns out to be no pig and all poke.

## Shill Bidding

When the seller or someone in association with the seller plants a phony bid to push up the price, this is called shill bidding. The shill has no intention whatsoever of buying the vehicle on the block. None of the other bidders are wise to the situation and continue to bid in good faith. When there is a false bidder in the crowd, this constitutes fraud.

## False Realities

Auction results are faithfully recorded in trade magazines and hobby newspapers. These results are used to calculate value guides. They are accurate in what they report, but because only a fraction of collectible automobiles are sold at auctions, the recorded results can give a distorted image of what a car is actually worth. Matt Joseph is an automotive historian who has been critical of the collectible car auction process for 30 years. He feels that auctions inflate the prices. He gives the example of a man who puts a Ford Model A on the auction block with a reserve of $25,000. The car gets to $20,000 but doesn't meet the reserve. The man has been offered less than $20,000 for the car since then but won't take it because in his mind it's worth that much. He knows so, because he saw that amount being bid with his own eyes. That $20,000 figure has become an artificial floor, a false reality.

Any vehicle is worth only what the market will bear and not one red cent more.

## Failure to Disclose

It can happen that the owner has not made full disclosure about the automobile's condition to the auction house. This can constitute breach of contract. I knew a man who bought a sweet 1960 station wagon that turned out to be stolen. Several months after he purchased his pride and joy, police seized the car. He wound up going to court to get his money back from the auction company.

Now you are familiar with a number of major reasons for not purchasing a collectible car at an auction. If you are uncomfortable with what you have read in this chapter, stop here and find another way to purchase your dream car. But if you're up for the challenge, you'll want to take a look at the next chapter.

**Meet Rob Myers — RM Auctions, Inc.**

Rob Myers was born in Chatham, Ontario, the youngest of four children belonging to Arsene and Rita Myers. Rob's dad, Arsene, was the maintenance man at Eaton Spring, a factory in town. Rob attended John McGregor Secondary School in Chatham and worked full time at Kmart, too. He dropped out of school in 1972 in the middle of grade twelve and quit his job at Kmart. He and a buddy took jobs where they could train to become certified welders. On the side, he did bodywork and painted cars. His cousin Ray Ouellette had a body shop in his backyard and worked there nights and weekends after shift work in the factory.

The first car that Rob remembers is a flathead Ford his dad tinkered with. He was always in the garage behind the house, helping his dad fix cars for family members. Rob was given a big black 1959 Edsel Corsair at age 13 when his dad upgraded to a 1968 Chrysler Newport. Rob spent the next two years gathering parts for the Edsel. He and his dad did the bodywork and painted it. They put the motor together and got it roadworthy for the big day when Rob turned 16 and got his driver's permit. He tooled around town with the Edsel for a week and promptly traded it for a 1970 Triumph Bonneville 650. Dad was upset about the deal for quite a while. Rob figured out soon enough that a motorcycle and a Canadian winter don't go together that well. For $1,000, he bought a 1940 Plymouth four-door sedan.

*Rob Myers with two of his business partners, Buck Kamphausen and Mike Fairbairn.*

Rob spent two years as a welder and had moved up to foreman by 1975. He was frustrated because the owner wouldn't sell him shares in the company. The best he could get was a commitment to think about it. Rob bought a new Harley Lowrider, stuffed some clothes into a knapsack, and decided to see the world. Well, North America, anyway. Three months and 35,000 miles later, Rob had seen much of Canada, the United States, and Mexico. Back home in Chatham, the owner wouldn't cut him into the company, so Rob quit.

Being a man with a plan, Rob decided to work full time in cousin Ray's garage and build up that business. Ray helped in the evenings and on weekends. Rob chuckles and says, "I am a workaholic. I got that work ethic from Dad, and I always will have it."

*The RM staff, circa 2004.*

*A 1938 Horch 853 Special Roadster. The restoration was performed by RM Auto Restoration and won the distinct honor of "Best of Show" at the 2004 Pebble Beach Concours d'Elegance.*

The business grew. So did Rob's interest in antiques and automobilia of all kinds. He and his dad collected gas pumps. To this day Rob is not 100 percent sure whether he is a collector or a pack rat, so he confesses to being a little bit of both. The collection was downsized considerably in 1979 when he decided to really grow the business and every penny counted. Even so, Rob's dad and brother Gerald co-signed for the 40-foot by 80-foot metal pole barn on the outskirts of town. When the deal was done, Rob remembers walking into the place and wondering what he would ever do with all that room. The answer was to fill it with work. Rob started by hiring one guy, and four years later, he had 15 employees.

Plenty of collision work on modern cars and collectible cars rolled into the shop as well. Rob had an excellent reputation, and customers trusted his work. Insurance adjusters didn't like to send work his way though because they were in the habit of getting freebies like minor repairs and having their cars washed and waxed. Rob didn't play those games. By 1983 insurance adjusters were a thing of the past; he was able to concentrate on his true love, the restoration of antique cars.

Rob's international reputation got a kick-start in 1983 when a customer from Sarnia, Ontario, wanted to buy a Duesenberg. Rob found a 1930 Town Car with a body by Murphy. It was owned by collector John Mozart but was in boxes and crates. Rob flew to California with a friend who was an expert in Duesenbergs. The car was a good deal. Rob brought it back to Canada and put it together for the customer. It took two years to bring the car back to life, and in 1985 the magnificent motorcar won Second in Class at Pebble Beach.

Rob met Cathy Van Raay, a modernist painter and sculptor, in the late 1970s. The two had actually attended high school together, but they didn't travel in the same circles and had never spoken. Rob remembers that on the first date he had to decide to pick her up either in a Corvette he had rebuilt from scrap or in a Lincoln. They got married in 1980.

Rob and Cathy have two children. Son Shelby is 22 and daughter Jessica is 21. Jessica clerks for the company, and Shelby is finishing his university degree. When the kids were little,

*Rob's business partner, Dan Spendick.*

Rob would take them on trips. He remembers that when Shelby was two they flew up to Ottawa to buy an Excalibur then drove it back to Chatham. Rob changed Shelby's diapers and gave him his bottle along the way. When Jessica was old enough, she traveled with her dad, too.

In 1986, Rob attended Fall Barrie, Canada's largest antique car show and swap meet. He was sitting there and read an ad about a guy who had a 1959 Cadillac Eldorado Barritz, a 1954 Packard Carribean, and a 1954 Caddy Eldorado convertible for sale. What stumped Rob was that the ad had a Chatham phone number, and those vehicles weren't any that Rob had ever seen. He got on the phone and met Dan Warrener who had moved to Chatham from Edmonton, Alberta. The cars were still in western Canada. Rob bought them over the phone. Dan's work was in Alberta. He collaborated with Rob by placing ads for antique cars. At one point, Rob was going out west every weekend and coming home with 20 to 30 cars. Dan came into the buying and selling business formally in 1987.

Mike Fairbairn joined the company in 1989. He had been vice president of sales for a computer company, and when he got a buyout, he was headed home to western Canada. He stopped in to see Rob on his way and wound up buying shares in the restoration business and settling in Chatham.

*Dan Warrener, Rob Myers, and Mike Fairbairn—the three amigos, circa 1997.*

Rob and Dan were buying and selling cars for themselves and for clients. They grew to be the biggest customer at other auctions. One year Rob recalls they took 134 cars to Kruse and between 60 and 70 to Barrett-Jackson. When they sat down and added it all up, they were taking between 300 to 450 cars to Kruse, Barrett-Jackson, Sotheby's, and Christie's. A lot of money was being paid out in commissions.

Late in 1990 the boys were attending Barrett-Jackson. They had dinner with Ernie Chapman and Dan Spendick who owned an auction company in Toronto. Ernie and Dan wanted to sell out. They all went back to the Roadway Inn and negotiated a deal on a table napkin while the four of them worked on a case of Labatt's Blue Light. Another big break came in 1996 when they bought Monterrey's sports car auction from Rick Cole in California. Rob is proud that the auction brought in $32 million in two evenings in 2006.

Mike Fairbairn wanted in on the auction deal, so they made a corporate decision to make Mike and Dan equal partners. Today RM boasts 80 employees. Each employee is a car nut and specialist. They know the hobby; they know the passion. Rob says, "We have grown our company with straight-ahead guys and no nonsense. Our handshake is gold; we treat people right. We have a good group of people around us." Rob notes that the folks at RM are young—the average age is in the thirties. The key to success for Rob is close ties to family and to staff that is like family.

The company has branched into private auctions and estate planning, and it has opened a new pop culture division with showrooms in Florida and Michigan. Pop culture memorabilia includes such names as Big Daddy Roth, Johnny Cash, and George Harrison. Today RM Auctions, Inc. does $250 million in business a year. The company operates the largest restoration shop in the world.

# 9 BEFORE YOU BID

## JOIN MAILING LISTS

Once you have identified auctions that are likely to be of interest, contact the people at the auction houses to place your name on their mailing lists. Once you are on those lists, you will receive advanced notice of when and where these auctions will be held. This permits you to plan for the purchase of your dream wheels in an unhurried manner. If you are going to attend a good-sized auction that is far away, inquire about hotel and even air travel packages. The staff at the auction house will be more than happy to answer your questions.

## PARTICIPATE IN AN AUCTION SEMINAR

Some auction houses offer free, get-acquainted seminars. In these sessions, newcomers are taught auction terminology and learn the lingo so they can take part with ease. They pick up the skills that permit them to bid properly and to buy successfully. They are also made aware of and taught how to deal with unusual situations that may arise at an auction. Folks who attend these sessions have a leg up on their competitors. When they arrive at an auction, their faces are already familiar to the staff, and they will pay special attention to them and help them with bidding.

*Sports Car Market* magazine subscribers have an "in" at Barrett-Jackson. They can ante up $300 for a two- or three-session on-site seminar before the auction. The first half of each day is spent hearing about the current market from Keith Martin, owner of the magazine. He shares tips about what's hot and what's not. Craig Jackson usually speaks at one seminar. These talks are followed by Field Block sessions, where the group goes outside to where the cars are actually being staged. An auction analyst leads various small groups in an examination of particular vehicles, showing them desirable characteristics to look for as well as defects and pitfalls to watch out for.

The 1971 Chevrolet Camaro is popular with collectors today.

## Take in an Auction as a Spectator

If a seminar is not available, it is a good idea to attend a couple of auctions and observe the operation first hand. Auction houses welcome this and, if you alert them in advance, they will often arrange for a staff member to personally guide you through the entire experience. There is generally no charge to watch an auction because you are not going to register to bid.

First off, you will note the three elements of the auction: the goods, the sellers, and the buyers. Then there is the auctioneer who orchestrates the proceedings. The auctioneer is assisted by ringmen who watch for bids. You will notice how the auctioneer and the bidders interact and develop a feel for the process. Attend several auctions run by different auctioneers and see how their styles vary. Aside from the entertainment and the fun, you will learn a great deal. Ask questions of folks who are experienced when you see something that you don't fully comprehend. Take notes!

Trial balloon auctions need not be automotive in nature. Weekly auctions of household goods and estate items are held in many communities. These are a good place to get your feet wet, and you may find yourself buying anything from Lladro figurines to antique lobster traps.

## Be an Early Bird

Don't wait until the auction starts to show up. Even though you are not participating, this is a full dress rehearsal! Give yourself plenty of time to examine the vehicles being sold. Take notes. You will want to match these personal notes against what the auctioneer says as the vehicles roll onto the block.

My father always said, "I would rather be an hour early than a minute late." That is sage advice and can be extremely critical at an auction event.

Entertainment is the number one reason that people attend auctions. Organizers know that and some of these events have become real extravaganzas with a genuine carnival-like atmosphere. Many open with all the pomp and circumstance they can muster. I get a genuine thrill at events that are kicked off with military honor guards and the national anthem. Lots of auction houses make use of upbeat music, like the theme from the movie *Rocky.* Auctioneers often get things underway by shouting to the crowd Michael Buffer's famous quote, "Are you ready to rumble?"

## Identify Yourself to the Auctioneer

If you have spoken to the auctioneer on the telephone but have not met, this is a good time to match the face to the voice. Take a few moments to introduce yourself and remind the auctioneer that this is your first auction. Be sure he or she knows you are observing, not participating. Establish a rapport. Ask where the auctioneer went to school, how long he or she has been in the business, and how today's auction will be run. Ask what items are expected to generate interest and run high.

Bidders are on the block to check out this 1967 Chevrolet Impala.

Auctions are conducted by sales and marketing professionals who carry the title of auctioneer. He or she asks for bids to establish an opening value. The auctioneer will continue to accept competitive, higher bids until there are no more. Then, the gavel falls to indicate the final hammer price.

## Watch the Crowd

Observe people's body language. If someone is hanging about a particular vehicle as if he or she already owns it, it is a sure sign the person is already emotionally attached to the car. This can be an indication that the individual is likely to overbid in order to own that vehicle. Find the vehicles that interest you, examine them dispassionately, and move on without drawing attention to yourself or your desire. Sometimes people present are quick to take note of "preowner behavior" and run up the bid a bit just to be aggravating.

Sometimes other bidders will stare, glare menacingly, or even make rude gestures at those who bid against them. This behavior is designed to intimidate and get others to stop bidding so that the coveted vehicle will be theirs.

## Let the Auction Begin!

The auctioneer walks out onto a raised stage or platform, sometimes called a podium. After introducing the staff and himself or herself, important announcements are made concerning the rules and regulations governing the sale. Announcements include the sale order, and while cars generally do not have any guarantees or warranties, occasionally a vehicle will have one and that will be noted. Other reminders will cover the taxes applicable, notification if the delivery date is different from the day of the sale, and any other noteworthy news.

Guarantees are few and far between, but sometimes there will be specific paperwork covering some aspect of a vehicle such as a freshly rebuilt engine that carries a warranty that is transferable to the new owner. A vehicle once owned by a celebrity will often be guaranteed to have documents of authenticity. These guarantees come from the owners or even manufacturers. No guarantees are ever offered by the auction firm.

The sale begins. An audible ripple of admiration rolls through the audience as the first set of dream wheels appears on stage, delivered by the ringman and crew. Everyone in the crowd is focused on the shining beauty, described in mouth-watering detail by the auctioneer, who opens the bidding. The auctioneer asks for an opening price. The person who is willing to pay a price will say it out loud and raise his card or paddle high so that it is noted. When noticed, the auctioneer will say, "You're in!"— meaning that the person is acknowledged as the opening bidder—or "You're out!"— meaning that the person must submit a higher bid in order to stay in the process.

Cars being readied for "the block" are prestaged in an area next to the auction platform entrance. Vehicles are consigned and each is given a lot number that is affixed to the windshield. A crew of drivers is on hand, and they drive the cars across the block in order. This ensures predictability and a steady stream of vehicles. Expect them to move at a rate of 20 per hour at an event held by RM Auctions, Inc., Kruse International, or the Barrett-Jackson Auction Company.

Ahead of time, make a note of the lot numbers of the vehicles you are interested in and then you can estimate when they will be brought to the staging area. Here is a chance to see the vehicles move under their own power.

Time the speed with which vehicles move across the block and calculate how far away from the stage your dream wheels are. The estimate will give you the opportunity to see your wheels in motion.

Sometimes the consecutive lot order progression is broken because a vehicle has been withdrawn at the last minute, the owner has become ill, or the car never made it to the auction venue. Generally, however, lot number order is religiously observed to bring continuity and convenience to the sale for all concerned.

## The Auctioneer

The auctioneer "calls" or "cries" the price of each bid. He or she recognizes bidders and the amount they have raised the bid. Finally, the auctioneer acknowledges the highest bidder and declares the close of the sale for a particular vehicle. In some areas, the auctioneer is alternatively known as the bid caller.

The auctioneer is a licensed professional who has graduated from an accredited school as a sales and marketing specialist. Many who are experienced at their craft receive certification from the Auctioneers Institute in the United States or the Institute of Canadian Certified Auctioneers. All auctioneers are obligated to practice their profession according to the code of ethics as decreed by the National Auctioneers Association Education Institute in the United States or the Auctioneers' Association of Canada. Membership in a professional association is voluntary, but it does inspire confidence in the consumer.

## The Ringman

Also known as the bid spotter, this staff member keeps an eagle eye on the audience, watching for fresh bids. Many auctions use more than one ringman. Most ringmen (yes, ringmen can be female) are often licensed auctioneers themselves but don't happen to be calling this particular event. The ringman's extra set of eyes and ears are of utmost importance to the auctioneer on the podium because it is often difficult to orchestrate bidding in a large crowd. The ringman will call out a loud "Yes!" or "Yup!" to let the auctioneer know the current asking bid has been met by a customer. The chant then moves upward to a new asking price.

## The Auctioneer's Patter

Auctioneers speak as fast as greased lightning. They do so because the flow of the patter and the momentum of their speech is a key component of the selling process. The auctioneer needs to zip right along because many vehicles will be auctioned off and people will lose interest if the sale begins to drag.

The chant provides a near magical environment that many look forward to and even demand while taking part in this type of business transaction. Occasionally the auctioneer will take a break from the distinctive singsong patter to make off-the-cuff comments, deliver a short speech, or tell a quick joke, all designed to warm up the audience as a means to encouraging folks to bid.

A good auctioneer is on the ball, leading bidders rather then being led by them. Highly skilled communicators, auctioneers are trained to read body language. They are constantly honing those skills to provide the "white heat" required to sell vehicles on the auction block.

Here we see cars lined up in the pre-staging area, readied for the trip to the auction block.

## Dissecting the Patter

There are three parts to the auctioneer's chant or call. The first part is a declaration of the current amount bid for the vehicle on the block. Second, there is some information given about the vehicle, provided to the auctioneer by the owner. This, in auctioneers' circles, is called "filler." It is always very rhythmic and is often highly colloquial in nature. If you should miss what is said here, don't worry; it is color commentary for the most part. The third part of the auctioneer's patter is an attempt to raise the current bid by asking for a higher one. "I've got five-five, who'll give me six?" means that the current price is $5,500, and the auctioneer is looking for $6,000, or an increment of $500. Once you get the hang of it, the patter is easy to understand and very enjoyable to the ears.

In most auctioneer schools, students will spend almost a third of class time developing a personalized chant. They are taught how to pace the rhythm of every word they say and speed of the cry. As well, they practice speaking "the call" with clarity. If an auctioneer can't be understood, there will be no sale.

Reflecting global interest in the hobby, the auction board shows the price for this 1970 Plymouth Superbird in US and Canadian Dollars, Pound Sterling, Yen, Euros, and Swiss Francs.

Savvy Tip

Language is particular and peculiar to the different regions of North America. The clipped speech of an auctioneer from the Maritime Provinces and the New England States will vary substantially from an auctioneer whose southern drawl is as big as Dixie. If you are not familiar with the accent, take time to acclimatize your ears before bidding.

## What the Auctioneer Sees

From the stage the auctioneer presides over a large crowd that can appear to be somewhat unruly. Those in attendance routinely turn around to chat with neighbors, whisper to each other, and sometimes even get up to walk around. The auctioneer is trained to spot the bidders who are raising those bid cards or paddles in the air. Serious bidders position themselves front and center, near the podium, so they can be clearly seen by the auctioneer. Cards rise and fall to the hypnotic rhythm of the polished patter, and the auctioneer never misses a beat. The bid climbs and so does the excitement.

## Bidding Increments

Auctioneers have set bidding increments to follow. Bids generally go up by $100 between $1,000 and $2,000, by $200 between $2,000 and $3,000, and increase by $1,000 when the bids reach from $10,000 to $20,000. Each house has its own pattern of bidding.

Once a bid hits the $100,000 mark, a hush will usually fall over the room. Bidders and non-bidders alike are interested, now. The increments jump quickly, and the air is filled with tension and excitement so thick that it can be cut with a plastic knife.

If you're not sure of the incremental increases, then ask. One major house uses the following increments for raising bids:

- 0 - 100 by 5
- 100 - 200 by 10
- 200 - 300 by 20
- 300 - 500 by 20, 50, 80 (i.e. 320, 350, 380)
- 500 - 1,000 by 50
- 1,000 - 2,000 by 100
- 2,000 - 3,000 by 200

- 3,000 - 5,000 by 200, 500, 800 (i.e. 4,200, 4,500, 4,800)
- 5,000 - 10,000 by 500
- 10,000 - 20,000 by 1,000
- 20,000 - 30,000 by 2,000
- 30,000 - 50,000 by 2,000, 5,000, 8,000 (i.e. 32,000, 35,000, 38,000)

Sometimes a bidder will shout out a number significantly higher than what is being called for at the present by the auctioneer. That bidder wants to be thought of as having a big or even an unlimited budget. This jumping strategy is designed to intimidate opponents.

## Half Bids

Another kind of bid trotted out on occasion is the "half bid." This occurs when the auctioneer is having trouble coaxing a higher bid out of the audience. A bidder may choose to raise the bid by only a half increment. A half-bid is only 50 percent of the increase the auctioneer is calling out. The bid may be at $25,000. The auctioneer will cry out, "I've got two-five, two-five, two-five. I've got two-five who will give me three?" He may do this several times, rapidly. If the bidding begins to look weak, the auctioneer may say, "Do it again!" He then repeats the process or says, "Don't lose the car for $5,000!" It can happen that a bidder will not want to raise the bid by the full five thousand and will pass a hand in front of his or her chest, palm down. This indicates a willingness to bid $27,500. The auctioneer may give the half bid a nod or choose to reject it.

## Raising the Stakes

As an observer at your first auction, you will note that interested parties may not open the bidding, but they do jump in early so the auctioneer knows they are interested in the vehicle currently on the block. Bidders hold their paddles or bid cards high so the auctioneer can see them. They make eye contact with the auctioneer to ensure their bid has been acknowledged. If the auctioneer should miss their bid, they shout it out, so they can stay in the process. Smart bidders keep an even tone of voice, so as not to give away their passion to own the vehicle and inadvertently alert others of their intentions. Once they have begun bidding, the auctioneer and the ringman will return to those active bidders to see if they are willing to bid higher.

At large auctions, television screens will show information about the vehicle on the block and display the current bid. The bid will also be shown converted into various currencies: U.S., Canadian, and Australian dollars, Euros, British Pounds Sterling, Swedish Kroner, and the Japanese Yen are common.

## Sometimes a Vehicle Is a No Sale

It has happened that two active bidders are in dead heat over a car, but the increments are slow. The auctioneer will suddenly move the vehicle off the block and commence calling for bids on the next lot number. This tactic adds an element of excitement to the sale and speeds the sale along. That car or truck may return later in the sale or be announced as having been sold off the block because the interested parties duked it out away from the stage area.

Brian Carlson has been part of the auction scene since 1990 as a reporter for *Old Cars*. He bought a 1974 Lincoln Continental Mark IV at a general auction in Minneapolis. The car was sold on consignment, one of four cars from an estate. The Lincoln went across the block as a "no sale" as the bidding only got up to $3,200 and did not meet the reserve. After the auction Brian was chatting with some people who had expressed some interest in the car and, in singing the Lincoln's praises, he inadvertently sold himself on the luxury boat! He then talked to the auctioneer and learned that the auction house held a late model car auction every month. Since Brian owned a late model Lincoln, he put down a deposit on the Continental Mark IV, sold his newer model at the next auction, and made a deal, straight across, with no commissions. The deal cost him a total of $200 all told.

## When It's Time to Bow Out

A bidder who wants to bow out because the price is higher than he or she wishes to pay simply indicates so by shaking the head in a "no" fashion very visibly when eye contact is made with the auctioneer. The auctioneer then looks elsewhere in the audience for higher bids. When a seasoned auction-goer has reservations of any kind about a particular vehicle, he or she will immediately pull out of the bidding process

## Reserve Prices

Vehicles are offered for sale either on a "Reserve" or "No-Reserve" basis. The reserve price is the minimum amount of money the owner will accept for the vehicle on the block. Cars without reserve generate a good deal of excitement because when the hammer falls, those vehicles will go home with the highest bidders, regardless of the final price.

On a vehicle that carries a reserve, the highest bid can fall below the required minimum amount. The owner is always encouraged to accompany a reserve vehicle to the block and stand with it while it is being auctioned off. If the real money comes close to the reserve, the auctioneer or ringman will encourage the owner to lower the reserve and complete the sale.

When that does not happen, the vehicle leaves the block as a "no sale." Often these cars are delivered to a post-sale area where prospective buyers have one more opportunity to examine and purchase the cars, even though they have already crossed the block.

When a reserve vehicle is sold after crossing the auction block, commissions are still collected by the auction house with accompanying paperwork processed through the office.

## Sold!

When the bidding has maxed out, the auctioneer will cry, "Going once! Going Twice! Sold!" The hammer comes down once that magic word is uttered; the clerk records the last bidder's number. Because the person has been aggressive in bidding, the hammer falls and the prize wheels go home with him or her. The successful bidder has been willing to pay the price in the bidding range. While other bidders were thinking in the same price range, the individual who bid last won the day.

Now that you have been to a seminar and/or observed an auction or two, it is time to focus on how to examine the vehicle you wish to buy.

# 10 EXAMINATION OF THE VEHICLE

The vast majority of vehicles sold at auctions are of good to superior quality. At a first tier auction, they are almost always at least Class Two in terms of condition. Some vehicles are even Class One. Regardless of condition, all vehicles are sold "as is." There is no guarantee, no warranty, no "cooling off" period in which one can return the purchase. That is why it is of utmost importance that the car or truck be carefully examined.

## Before You Go

When perusing the auction house catalog or Web site usually more than one snazzy number catches your eye. Call the auction house to make sure that particular vehicle is on site before going to inspect it. Sometimes owners will withdraw their cars or even sell them ahead of time. Don't make a trip for nothing and be disappointed.

Arrive early so that you can check out the cars in an unhurried manner. Safety and insurance rules dictate that potential purchasers are not permitted to drive the cars but are allowed to check them out before bidding. You may hear the engine run. Bring along a mechanic or other expert if you wish; they're more than welcome. If you can't hear the engine run, do establish that the vehicle has at least one set of keys. You may be chuckling now, but you won't be should you discover that the vehicle you have just bought is going to cost you an extra $500 to have a set of keys made.

Keys are often tied to the steering column. Some auction houses make use of a Key Control person, one assigned to each lot number.

## Ask Good Questions

Keep in mind that the owner is as anxious to sell as you are to buy. As a serious bidder have a quiet word with the auction house and, if at all possible, staff will arrange for you to meet with the owner, either at the auction or beforehand. Meeting the owner beforehand is preferable; you won't be rushed. Most owners are almost always happy to talk about their cars. Ask specific questions. Never ask a general question such as, "Is there anything wrong with the car?" Be specific. Use focused, targeted questions such as: "May I see the compression test?" or "Can you show me the bill for the last alignment?"

Some statements don't mean anything. When a widow tells you that her husband was the only one who ever drove it, you have learned nothing about his driving skills or habits. On the other hand, some statements tell volumes. This statement—" It doesn't have any rust, we had it all fixed"— is an indication that the tin worm is present. Experienced collectors know that unless the car has undergone a frame-off restoration, the old axiom, "once rusty, always rusty" rings true.

Spend as much time assessing the car's owner as you do the car that is up for auction. You will learn volumes about the car as you assess the owner's answers to your questions.

When preparing a vehicle for viewing at the auction site, the wise owner will remove easily stolen parts and set them aside for safekeeping. These will include small items like gearshift knobs, radio control knobs, and cigarette lighters. On older vehicles, those magnificent radiator caps are genuine works of art and can be irreplaceable. Inquire, should you note things missing. You don't want to buy the vehicle and then find out too late that those hard-to-find items have indeed actually been stolen or were missing all along.

Do bring a pair of coveralls and get underneath the vehicle to examine its underside. Study the frame, the cross members, and floor pans for cracks, damage, and rust. If there are leaks, determine what they are and where they come from. Rusty brakes, for example, can indicate prolonged storage. Check the exhaust system.

Sometimes cars have been altered. I once took a nice Rambler to my mechanic for inspection. He put it up on the hoist and, to his horror, discovered that the gas line had been moved so that it ran directly under the exhaust system. With any extended use at all, a potentially deadly explosion and fire would have occurred. Another car I drooled over had been given a homemade brake rebuild by the owner. It wasn't a very good job, and it would have cost $2,000 to restore them to proper working order.

The doors, the hood, and the trunk should all open and close easily. Run the heater and the air conditioner. Tires that are bald or show signs of uneven wear indicate alignment problems at the least and may possibly indicate an accident that bent the frame or twisted the unit body. Examine the wheel rims for damage. Write down and check the serial numbers. A cell phone call to a friend with computer access or a Blackberry comes in mighty handy in verifying the numbers.

Savvy Tip

When previewing vehicles, bring along a camera, a flashlight, a magnifying glass, mirror, a pen, and a small notebook so you can take notes. On the day of the auction use those notes and images to refresh your memory as you make a second inspection to ensure that the vehicles are in the same condition as when last inspected.

## Frame-Off Restoration

When you learn that a vehicle has undergone a frame-off restoration, it means that literally every piece of the machine has been disassembled and restored to "like new" condition before being rebuilt. Although it seems a little silly, the term is used even when the vehicle is of monocoque or unit construction and never had an actual frame.

## Blueprinted Engine

This restoration term is used to define an engine that has been rebuilt and tuned to original factory specifications. It may not be terribly pertinent to a 1961 Chevrolet Biscayne six-banger, but it can be critical information when you are in the market for a V-8 muscle car once piloted by the Hell Drivers or a NASCAR racing legend.

## Engine Checks

Restored or not, you will want to determine the compression reading in each cylinder by using a compression tester. The procedure does take some time but is a wise precaution. An engine rebore is costly. A cracked block or cracked head for that 1930 Chrysler may cost a bundle or even be impossible to source. Look for oil leaks under the car. Check the oil pressure while the engine is running. Run the engine long enough to determine whether or not it overheats. If the car is old enough, its carburetor will be made of pot metal. You will have a tough time locating another if this one is in bad repair. Soft spongy hoses and frayed, ratty-looking wires are easy enough to replace.

A man I know bought a 1930 Ford Model A coupe. The oil pressure gauge was erratic and numerous efforts to repair it didn't work. A new gauge didn't do the trick, either. Finally, the exasperated mechanic told the owner he had fixed it, and the gauge would never bother him again. The owner was as pleased as punch until he got into the Ford and saw the mechanic's solution—he had painted the oil pressure gauge black!

Watch the exhaust as it comes out of the pipe; it speaks volumes about the engine. Remove the air filter and examine what has collected there. You may find watermarks in the engine bay that indicate the vehicle has been through a flood. The starter should not grind, and the engine should not ping or knock. All fluids should be clean and fresh. If there are maintenance stickers present, compare them with mileage on the odometer. Significant engine problems will significantly lower the vehicle's value.

The 1930 Chrysler 66 Brougham was good value when new and still is today.

Savvy Tip

If you intend to license and drive your car in California, it is important to run a Gross Polluter Check before purchasing. A vehicle that has failed an emissions test in the Golden State is branded a "Gross Polluter." It must be brought up to standard before it can be certified. That proposition can break the bank.

## Air-Conditioning

While under the hood, check the air-conditioning system components for structural integrity and examine it for leaks, too. If it is not blowing cold—just blowing air—there may be a problem. An air conditioner thermometer placed in the cabin outlet vents is an effective measure of coldness. Since my 1969 Ambassador was a daily driver, I had the Freon changed over to the environmentally safer R134A coolant at a cost of $1,600.

The most commonly smuggled contraband item into the United States from Canada is not drugs or weapons; it is Freon. The reason is because the coolant is still made in Canada, but its manufacture has been phased out in the United States.

## Transmission, Clutch, and Differential

Again, check for leaks under the parked vehicle. If you are lucky enough to be permitted to drive the car, remember, a two-speed Borg Warner automatic from the 1950s is never going to shift as smoothly as today's cars, not by a long shot. You can expect some jerkiness and that is perfectly acceptable for cars of that era. Transmission troubles can be complex and expensive or as simple as a disconnected hose. A rebuild will set you back a good $1,500 depending on the vehicle. Some transmissions are just plain finicky. A 1955 Packard equipped with the shelf-shifting Ultramatic unit will cost you an arm and quite possibly a leg too, when the time comes for repairs.

It is strictly forbidden to bring tools to an auction site and use them on a vehicle.

My grandmother's 1963 Studebaker Standard came with a three-speed manual transmission. It had the annoying habit of locking up between first and second gear. The problem was never resolved, but I became quite adept at hopping out of the car at red lights, even in city traffic, and hitting the linkage with a wrench to free it. The car would shift fine for a while and then inexplicably seize up, again. The linkage and its components are almost always repairable or replaceable. I never did repair it because hopping out and smacking the linkage always impressed dates!

## Interior

Roll the windows up and down. They should not be loose, hard to operate, or be crooked. Power windows should work smoothly. Pull every knob and flick every switch. The rocker switches on those 1963 to 1966 Studebakers can be very touchy. Turn on the lights and leave them on for a while to see if they operate properly or short out. Test the emergency brake. Check for water stains that may indicate past leaks, and look for telltale traces of sealant used to stop those leaks. Sniff for a damp, musty smell. Take a mirror and look under the seats. If you find mold or springs that are rusty, the car may have survived a flood.

Look under the carpet for signs of rust or mold. Upholstery and carpeting are easy enough to replace. There are companies that cater specifically to this need. I have used one in Oregon and another in New Jersey with satisfying results. Some restoration companies actually have new old stock (NOS) on hand.

The 1955 Packard Caribbean Convertible was beautiful but its poor quality guaranteed poor sales.

If the vehicle under consideration has new carpet for no apparent reason, it can be an indication that the floor rotted through or the car was submerged in water.

It is a snap to find interior paint these days. Computers can make perfect matches. What is often difficult to find are trim items. In the 1960s, plastics came into widespread use. Often these early plastic parts weren't up to the job. More than once I have unearthed difficult to find NOS plastic trim and installed them, only to have them break, too.

Henry Ford was first to bring plastics into the automobile's interior. He believed that farmers should share in the prosperity of the automobile industry and sought crops that could be used in automobile manufacturing. Ford scientists hit pay dirt with soybeans. They found a multitude of uses for the lowly legume, including plastic. Tens of thousands of acres of soybeans were grown by farmers at Henry's request and the Ford Motor Company sowed more than 20,000 acres, too. The first production automobile to incorporate plastic in an appreciable way was the 1938 Ford, boasting 11 pounds of the miracle product. To prove that plastic was durable, Ford brought in the press to show off a 1940 Ford with exterior panels made completely of soybean-based plastic. He took a sledgehammer to the trunk, but it merely bounced off, leaving no dent.

## The Trunk

Lift up the rubber matting in the trunk and look carefully for holes or rust. If there is dampness or a musty smell, there is a leak somewhere. Remove the spare tire from the well and check carefully. Tap the walls and listen for a sloshing sound. Water can get trapped in the inner fender wells and collect there.

## The Body and Exterior Trim

When examining a car, beware of new shiny paint. Old, original paint is better. New paint can cover a multitude of things. An untouched original is the most desirable of all vehicles. Original paint is baked onto the shell in a giant oven, not sprayed and left to air dry.

Take a long, critical look at the sheet metal. This is the part of your vehicle that folks will see most. It should be in the best of shape. Use a strong, portable light to cast shadows on the body panels. If the lines are not smooth but wave or have an uneven, watery look, it is likely that extensive bodywork has been performed on the vehicle. If that appears to be the case, gently place a magnet on the surface. The magnet should adhere to the car. If it does not, filler, such as Bondo, has been used to repair the surface.

Ken Buttolph has been going to auctions for years. He has seen cars with bodywork so bad the bodywork bulged like a bag of walnuts. He quips that he has seen his share of "friendly cars"—cars with substandard bodywork will "wave" at you. If you're looking at a 1967 Olds and it has enough waves on the body to make you seasick, you ought to move on to another car.

Experienced auction-goers often bring along an Elcometer. This digital device measures paint thickness. When the indicator reaches eight to 12 millimeters, it indicates a paint job or even bodywork has been performed on the car.

Doors must line up. Hinges may show signs of rust. Cars with tired unit bodies may have doors that droop significantly. Check carefully around the door openings and places where rubber and felt meet metal or glass for signs of paint overspray. No matter how carefully the car has been prepped, there is almost always some telltale overspray. This is highly significant in lowering the value if you have been told that the car is completely original.

Sheet metal, fenders, doors, felts, and rubbers are almost always replaceable. So are convertible tops. One exception seems to be station wagon tailgates and hatchback doors. If the tailgate or hatch is in poor shape, don't count on being able to find NOS parts or remanufactured parts. Be prepared to track down a good one from a donor car or commence a complete rebuild of the one you have now.

As you examine the trim, take careful note that it is held down securely with clips. I have seen double-sided tape be used in their absence, even screws. When a tractor hit my prized Ambassador wagon, it needed extensive repairs. The body shop people lost some of the clips and I nearly cried when I discovered the tailgate's red reflector panel had been bolted on. Once when loading a car onto a trailer, the right rear wheel suddenly went flat. Upon examination it was discovered that a trim piece had been fastened to the body with a screw so long that it dug into the tire and punctured it!

One of the most satisfying ways to get to know a vehicle is to take it on a date and treat it to a bucket of hot, soapy water. There is nothing more satisfying than washing a car from stem to stern. As you wash and rinse, you get to know every surface of the car's body.

## Restoration or Hurry-Up Job?

There is a world of difference between a careful restoration and shoving a car through the shop with a substandard hurry up job. Ken Buttolph recalls a horrific scene at one auction. A seller had a large number of 1957 Chevrolets lined up in a row. The paint on these cars was so fresh the smell filled the air. As the cars were headed for the block, a frantic worker was pulling wheel covers out of a bushel basket and pounding them onto the wheels as the cars were being rolled onto the stage!

This gorgeous modified 1957 Chevrolet goes by the name Chezoom. It fetched $372,600 on the auction block.

## Keep Notes

As you examine the vehicles that interest you, take extensive notes of repairs needed. These notes will be immensely helpful as you calculate the maximum price you are willing to bid. Checking your notes is easier than relying on your memory. Using this simple technique will save you much grief as the vehicles appear on the block.

## When You Cannot Physically Inspect the Vehicle

It may happen that you are unable to physically inspect the vehicle yourself. You can request a condition report from the auction house. If one is available, it will be forwarded to you. Since some vehicles will be off site, a condition report may not be ready until a few days before the sale date.

Once you have finished examining the vehicle, move away. Hanging around needlessly after your examination will tip your hand to potential competitors that you are interested in this particular vehicle. It may drive up the price when the bidding starts.

### Meet Spanky and Amy Assiter — America's Royal Auctioneer Couple

**Spanky Assiter**

Born and raised in Floydada, Texas, Tommy, better known as Spanky, Assiter was the middle of three children. His dad was a life insurance agent. Spanky was a very private child who liked to stay alone in his room. He has fond memories of going to auctions run by the Future Farmers of America and 4-H. He and his brother raised pigs to enter in the competitions, and during the high school years, sheep were added to the mix. His family turned up often at other stock shows and farm sales, too. Spanky remembers that the atmosphere at auctions was charged with excitement, and he was always ready to go to one and watch the animals get sold.

Square dancing was a popular activity in Floydada, and Spanky went to the Saturday night dances with the family at the junior high school gym. Like all the other kids, he learned to dance, but then he discovered he had a knack as a caller. By the time he was 12 he was calling the dances at the high school gym. A radio station in Oklahoma City broadcast square dance music after midnight on Saturdays. Spanky was glued to the radio for the entire broadcast. A popular tune entitled the "Auctioneer's Song," written and performed by LeRoy Van Dyke, was turned into a square dance number.

That song had quite an impact on Spanky. Upon graduation from high school in 1975, he headed off to learn auctioneering at the World Wide College of Auctioneering in Mason City, Iowa. He learned that if an item could carry a price tag and be taxed by the government it was likely to turn up on an auction block one day. He was taught to sell antiques, livestock, cars, and real estate. More than that, he learned how to handle general auctions, estate auctions, and farm auctions.

*Spanky at Keeneland*

Auctioneer school wasn't the end of the educational road. Spanky's dad wanted all his children to have a university education, and they did. Spanky graduated from West Texas A&M in 1979 in Canyon, Texas, with a B.S. in Speech. His concentration was in Mass Communications. He received his M.B.A. at the same institution in 1981.

Spanky, like every other auctioneer, developed his own unique chant at school. He liked the Western Style and made it his bid calling style. This chant is popular in North America and makes him highly sought after. Spanky is one of the few auctioneers in the business who can switch from collector cars to wholesale cars to horses to real estate to farm sales with ease.

The Western Style gives Spanky the speed and clarity to do a good job. Just like a good baseball pitcher has a variety of pitches, Spanky learned to change up or vary his patter. "The variety is part of the sales technique that creates excitement," he says.

He is proud of the clarity of his patter as well. His auction chant contains no "rubbish." He explains "rubbish" in his own words. "An auction chant has three parts. The first is the statement—what the bid is. The second is the suggestion—what you want the bid to be. The third part of the chant is the question—will you give $20?" Spanky shares. "The question gets faster and faster as it is repeated. Some auctioneers don't repeat the question when they get going fast. They just make a drubbing noise."

At a wholesale auto auction, 40 to 50 vehicles an hour cross the block. At an auto factory sale, where cars are sold only to dealers, it's even faster. As many as 150 to 200 vehicles cross the block in a single hour at a factory sale. "That's a lot of tongue revolutions per minute," laughs Spanky. At a big auction like Kruse or Barrett-Jackson, the pace is much more leisurely. Collector cars cross the block at a rate of 20 per hour.

All that talk wreaks havoc on an auctioneer's voice. Just as athletes keep their bodies in prime condition, an auctioneer's voice must be worked out and cared for so as not to damage it. Spanky avoids coffee as much as possible. Before an auction, he warms up his voice by humming then moves on to voice drills, rhythm drills, and tongue twisters. One of his favorites is "Betty Botter bought some butter, but she said this butter's bitter. If I put it in my batter, it will make my batter bitter. So she bought a bit of better butter, put it in her bitter batter, made her bitter batter better, so 'tis better Betty Botter bought a bit of better butter." Spanky says that this drill is excellent for developing rhythm and the flow to a chant.

*A Brashears Auction*

A stint can be as long as nine hours in a day. There is an enormous strain on the vocal chords, and great care is taken so that the auctioneer does not lose it altogether. At big events, five or six auctioneers spell each other off, usually selling 10 to 20 vehicles at a time before taking a break.

Spanky decided to become a full-time auctioneer in 1983 and has never looked back. He has won many auctioneering competitions. In 1991 he took grand prize in the International Auctioneer Championship sponsored by the National Auctioneers Association (NAA).

He started calling for Barrett-Jackson in 1992. There he worked with Amy. One of his buddies told him if Spanky didn't marry her that somebody else would make her rich. That set Spanky to sparking, and he and Amy tied the knot on Valentine's Day in 2004. As happy as they can be, they make their home in Canyon, Texas. They are active in their church, and the three kids get along fine in their newly blended family.

Spanky collects clowns. He has prints, artwork, and figurines in blown glass, papier mache, and silver to name just a few. He has loved clowns since he was a kid. One thing that he always wanted to do was learn to tie balloons into the shapes of animals, like clowns do. He spotted a man doing that at the airport one day, and on the plane, Spanky introduced himself to Craig Davis who taught him how it's done. The two of them have become great friends.

In 2004, after a series of dizzy spells, Spanky was diagnosed with a brain tumor that pressed on his optic nerve. The surgery was successful but bright lights hurt his eyes. The doctor offered to do something about the eyes, but Spanky fixed the problem himself with "cheaters," those magnifying glasses you can buy at the drugstore. The specs have become his trademark. In 2005 Spanky won the World Automobile Auctioneers' Championship for the second time, a year to the day after the brain cancer surgery. The four-foot-tall trophy has a place of honor in the office.

**Amy Assiter**

Amy Paul grew up smack dab in the middle of Oklahoma in Garvin County. She can trace her heritage back to the British Isles and is a proud citizen of the Chickasaw Nation, too. She attended cattle auctions with her grandfathers and remembers how much she looked forward to hanging out with them in the sales barn and listening to the music of the auctioneers' patter.

Blessed with a beautiful voice, Amy sang her way through high school in the show choir. Her talent won her a spot in the National Band and Chorus USA in 1987. The group performed for folks in such exotic venues as Hawaii, Australia, and New Zealand. Amy didn't just sing. She had a flair for drama too and displayed her talent in school plays and musicals. She loved participating in extemporaneous speaking and prepared speech contests and even did a little debating. Amy graduated from Stratford High in 1988. She continued to sing at galas and Remington Park, a race track in Oklahoma City. She sang in both religious circles and public venues.

Settling on a career as a commodity broker, she handled currencies, metals, agricultural commodities, and the cattle that went out from the stockyards in Oklahoma City. Restless by nature, she didn't particularly like sitting behind a desk. It became a ball and chain, and Amy began to think about escaping the confines of the office.

She knew the auctioneers around town because her firm did business with them. Ralph Wade, a world champion livestock auctioneer, offered to teach Amy the auction business. She thought about it and a few months later took him up on his offer.

The singing background gave her a jump-start. She already knew how to breathe and how to project her voice. She had a strong sense of rhythm and was at ease in front of audiences. Auctioneering was a natural progression for the singer. Within a year, she was on the block, and in 1999 she won the Oklahoma State Auctioneers Association's Rookie Championship. Winning that contest definitely put her career on the map.

Amy's first gig as a professional auctioneer still makes her laugh. She went to Ada, Oklahoma, for a sale. The boss handed her the warm-up. Amy auctioned off bags of pecans, live rabbits and chickens, eggs, animal crates, and cages. When the crowd was warmed up, sheep and goats were trotted out.

In 2000 she went to Norfolk, Virginia, where she won the International Auctioneer Championship sponsored by the NAA. Within three years, she had carved a huge name for herself in the industry. Being a woman in a male-dominated industry didn't hurt one bit.

She began teaching the intricate craft to students at the World Wide College of Auctioneering in Mason City, Iowa, in 2002. Amy taught seminars in Chant Structure and

*Amy and Spanky with his World Automobile Auctioneers' Championship trophy and his trademark specs.*

Client Communication Guidelines. These students were generally not fresh-faced teenagers; the average age was 45, and they had all come to fulfill a lifelong dream.

Amy joined the Barrett-Jackson team in 2003 as a ringman or bidder assistant. Stationed on the stage at the back end of the vehicle up for bid, she will watch as few as three and as many as 100 potential bidders at a time. She has a sharp eye. That hammer will come down in three minutes or less! Another one of her pleasant duties at the Scottsdale, Arizona, extravaganza is to open the event by singing "The Star-Spangled Banner."

A longtime and wise observer of human nature, Amy comments, "Auction competition between buyers can be downright funny. They can get cocky and competitive. Some can be quite wild." She recalls one bidding war where a man was so excited that she had to pull him off the car that was up for bid and almost had to separate him from his competitor. He kept yelling that his competitor didn't have enough money to outbid him. In the ensuing frenzy, the two inadvertently drove the price of the car to $3 million, plus the premium!

Amy says, "Auctioneers know their market whether it is cars, horses, or something else, but it is more important that the auctioneer know the people." She adds, "The thrill is an adrenaline high. The fast pace is full of energy; it's an addictive atmosphere." Amy loves the people she meets. They come from every walk of life, and she enjoys working with them.

Amy and Spanky successfully juggle their careers and a home life with three daughters and three dogs: a Great Pyrenees named Sulley, a Jack Russell named Boo, and a Sun Conure named Tie-Dyed. Everybody pitches in to help keep the household running smoothly. Folks often ask the girls if their parents talk fast at home. The girls' deadpan response is always, "Oh, yeah, and you should hear them when they get into an argument!"

Amy has cut back on her extensive traveling and works only at select venues these days. This gives her more time to spend with her family and to be active in their church. A writer, she is working on a series of children's storybooks with a Native American theme.

# 11 YOUR FIRST AUCTION

## Dress for Success

Clothes make the bidder! Dressing in such a manner that gives you the appearance of being an individual with some means at your disposal will prompt other bidders to take notice of you in a positive light. They will certainly evaluate you in a much different way than if you show up in a baggy sweatshirt, torn jeans, and sandals. No one expects you to be a fashion plate or a clothes horse but wearing the right clothing does bring respect and, as such, can mean the difference between being the high bidder or not.

If you have chosen to participate in a posh, upscale gala event, familiarize yourself with the dress code and make the appropriate preparations well in advance. Tuxedos and ball gowns require specific accessories, so plan accordingly. If the vehicle you intend to purchase is an integral part of your business strategy, money spent on fancy dress may be tax deductible.

Most auction houses suggest business casual as the recommended attire. For men that means slacks, loafers, shirt without tie, and sometimes a sports jacket. For women, business casual means office wear, certainly nothing provocative. People who attend auctions tend to be fairly conservative in beliefs, dress, and manner. It is a bad mistake to irritate other bidders needlessly by dressing in clothing that will stand out or offend. Inappropriate attire can have an astonishingly negative impact, causing folks to bid against you simply to make sure you don't go home with the prize.

I recall one auction held for an international charity. While most of the folks were dressed conservatively, one couple arrived wearing so little and dressed in such a provocative fashion, blind nudists would have blushed. Everyone present gave the flashy couple wide berth, and they were the cruel butt of more than one crude joke. Although the scantily clad pair acted like serious auction-goers, they went home empty handed that day because the other bidders closed ranks out of pure hostility and consistently outbid them.

### Dress Appropriately for Mother Nature

If the auction you have chosen to attend is to be held out of doors, make sure you have the necessary clothes to make the day enjoyable. You may want to take along a sweater, mitts, headgear, raincoat, even boots if the forecast indicates that the weather will turn cold, pour buckets, or be muddy. There is nothing worse than being miserable, wet, or cold. Almost all physical discomfort is preventable with a little foresight. Umbrellas protect against sun and rain. Headgear and sunscreen are wise precautions.

Attendance at an auction is often lower in very hot, cold, or inclement weather. Chances are increased when fewer people turn out.

## Bring Food and Beverages

Most auctions feature on-site food vendors. If the fare is not to your liking, bring your own, after finding out it is permissible. Never bring alcohol, but do bring plenty of water to prevent dehydration.

## Bring a Friend

Having a trusted friend at your side will help you to stay anchored, so that you don't get carried away in the heat of the moment. Make sure the friend is completely unflappable. Let

Specialty cars like TV's Batmobile always draw a crowd.

the friend know your strategy and spending limit. Make sure your friend doesn't wander off. I know a man who had no intentions of buying anything and had a friend along to keep him sane. The friend went to the washroom and, in those few short minutes, his errant buddy managed to buy a car he didn't even want!

## Preregistration

Most houses encourage clients to pre-register. Some of the bigger ones require it and enforce a mandatory 48-hour cutoff point before the sale takes place. Even if you are pre-registered, on auction day you still must identify yourself at the cashier's office or registration area and fill out the necessary paperwork in order to receive your bid card or paddle.

The bigger the auction event, the smarter it is to preregister. A large show will draw as many as 6,000 bidders, and the lines can be long.

## Registration

If you have not already registered, do so now. Bring proper identification including proof of identity, current address, and telephone number. A passport, driver's permit, a letter of credit from the bank, pertinent bank information, and credit card should suffice. Applications are scrutinized thoroughly to weed out scamsters and con-artists. You will be given a paddle or card printed with your personal sale number. You will note that many others have client numbers. A client number is not important the first time around, but if you become a regular, a permanent number shortens the registration process considerably because all your necessary information is already on file. Some of the more prestigious firms offer exclusive client cards to speed things along.

A letter of credit from your bank may be required in order to bid. A big auction event like Barrett-Jackson will have more than a billion dollars worth of credit authorization on hand for a single show.

If you are exempt from paying taxes, at this time you must complete a Certificate of Exemption and give proof of your tax exemption number.

## Ask Questions

While registering, take time to find out how the sale will be conducted. Ask if there is a Buyer's Premium on the vehicles you are interested in. If there is, calculate that into the price you are willing to pay The buyer's premium is the percentage that the auction house adds to the hammer price. It contributes to their profit line. Inquire at this time if there are any restrictions on the vehicles you want. It can happen that a vehicle is sold for export only. If that is the case, find out if you are exempt from sales tax. That may be the case if you live in a different jurisdiction than the one in which the sale takes place. You may be given a tax claim form to fill out. Find out when the vehicle must be removed, if you're the successful bidder. Ask if there is a surcharge for paying with a credit card. This information will need to be calculated into your budget.

## Final Inspection

Arrive plenty early to make sure your vehicle is in the same condition it was when you looked it over during the pre-auction inspection. If it isn't, you will want to speak to a ringman or even the owner to find out what has happened. Make some quick recalculations to establish the top price you are willing to pay, if you want it at all, now.

It can happen that the vehicle you have your heart set on has been damaged or even withdrawn from the auction. It is wise to have researched several vehicles so that you have a range to bid on.

## Location! Location! Location!

Stake out a seat somewhere near the podium so the auctioneer or the ringman can spot you easily. Take a good look at the other bidders to see how they are dressed and what vehicles appear to be of interest to them.

## A Word to the Auctioneer

Before the auction begins, speak to the auctioneer and the ringman. They will be readily identifiable; the team will often wear distinctive blazers or caps and badges. Let them know which vehicle you are interested in. Because you have done your homework thoroughly, you know exactly what you are willing to pay for vehicles in your area of interest. Make sure the auctioneer and the ring crew knows that, too. They will pay particular interest to you when that car or truck crosses the block.

An auctioneer must have extremely sharp eyes.

Ringmen are strategically placed auction crew who assist both the auctioneer and bidders. These people clearly call out current bids to the auctioneer and, more importantly, serve to guide you during the fast paced bidding process. As prices are being called and bidding is fierce, a ringman is a valuable ally in keeping track where the bidding is. It is wise to establish a good relationship with your ringman to attain the car of your dreams.

## Become a Regular

Being recognized by the auctioneers as a regular works greatly to your advantage. You grow more comfortable and confident with repeated experience. When your face is familiar and your tastes are known, the staff will alert you to vehicles that may very well be of interest.

Don't waste the time of those helping you by asking about vehicles you have no real interest in purchasing.

## The Warm-Up

Some of the bigger auctions don't start by placing automobiles on the block. At Barrett-Jackson, the show starts early in the morning, and the audience needs a little warm-up at that hour. While the vehicles are on hand for all to see, first on the block are beautiful examples of automobilia. For a good hour or more auctioneers offer gas station signs, vintage gas pumps, pedal cars, race posters, furniture made from automobiles, and automotive literature. Each lot is carefully placed in an order to excite those in attendance. When the crowd is red-hot and rarin' to go, then the automobiles and trucks are offered to bidders.

Automobilia is a vast area of collecting. Some folks limit themselves to gas station signs or gasoline pumps.

## Opening Bid

Once your dream wheels are on the block, it is not necessary to open the bidding. Being first can tip your hand that you are keen to own the vehicle. Let someone else establish the bottom price.

## Bidding Early

While you may not bid first, do bid early to confirm your interest. Seasoned bidders usually join in after the second or third bid. Some will wait longer. They wait because they want to see exactly what the interest is and to get a feel for how the crowd reacts to this particular vehicle.

If you wish to remain anonymous, it is a good tactic to bid big one time then use a secret, prearranged signal with the auctioneer to continue.

## Bidding Pattern

Watch the other bidders closely. Once the bidding is moving along smoothly, raise your paddle and call out a conservative bid of your own. Raise it high, that's why you have it. Don't call out your paddle number either, that will confuse things further. If you're missed, shout "Yes!" The auctioneer will recognize your bid and by gum, you're in! Don't be a wallflower at an auction. This is aggressive buying, and you must make certain that your intention to bid is recognized by the house. Deliberate confident bids send a clear message to other prospective bidders and to the auctioneer. Your bidding pattern lets all parties present know that you are serious about this vehicle. The auctioneer will come back to you time and time again for a higher bid, having established that you are desirous of taking this set of wheels home with you.

Sometimes a heated battle will break out between two bidders. The auctioneer will concentrate on them, taking bids until one drops out. Then the auctioneer turns to the whole audience to best the current bid.

You cannot remove your vehicle from the premises until the auction house has approved your financial arrangements.

Now that you're in, pay no attention to the competition. Keep your eyes fixed on the auctioneer and the prize. Stay calm and focused. Don't fall into the trap of being intimidated by other bidders who may mutter, glare at you, and even cuss in hopes of getting you to stop bidding against them. If you are on the block looking at the car, don't engage in a face-off with a competitive bidder. Don't show off for the crowd or draw attention to yourself. You came to buy a vehicle not entertain the audience.

Stand up, yell, shout, and wave your card if you feel that you are being missed. Some auctioneers take bids from only two people and when one drops out will only then go to another bidder. You can always point to yourself, and the auctioneer will tell if you are in or out.

The competition is between those who are bidding seriously. These people are laying down "real money" for the vehicle on the block. While you are keeping your eyes on the auctioneer or the ringman, keep one eye on the competition, too.

## Bow Out Gracefully

Stick to your price and keep a cool head. Keep out of any emotionally charged bidding wars. Don't bid one cent more than planned when you calculated your initial strategy. Should the bidding pass your top dollar price, shake your head "no," and let others do battle over the car or truck. If you're angry, don't let it show. Nobody appreciates a sore loser.

Overbidding is the most common mistake that beginners make. Those dream wheels are no longer a bargain the minute the bid goes over the top price you are willing to pay.

## Buying Times

Optimal times to buy are early in the auction and late at night. If half the crowd has left for dinner, you will have a better chance of getting a bargain. Familiarize yourself with the peak times and low periods at auctions.

Study the distinctive ebb and flow of the crowd's enthusiasm. Auctions tend to thin out as the day wears on. Auction prices are higher in the mornings, after the breakfast crowd has come into the arena and warmed up. Sometimes a car that has been run through early in the morning and didn't sell will be run through a second time. Often the first 25 cars will shine for a second time on the block. The crowd will be largest—and the bidding most fierce—from noon to 4 o'clock on Saturday. That is when the folks with the biggest cash wads are there, and that is when the most desirable cars are run across the block.

If it is too hot, too cold, or too windy, there will be fewer participants. Late Friday night and at the end of the show, there is somewhat less competition. There are still good bargains to be had at the end of an auction because many have gone home. However, that is not as true as it was 10 years ago because dealers have noticed that too and taken advantage of the situation. They did not come to buy with the intention of reselling those bargain wheels elsewhere, but the bargains were too good to pass up.

Savvy Tip

When an event is spread over several days, study it carefully to find where your car will be positioned in the sale. Some auction houses want to build up momentum all the way to the end of the sale; others start with the best offerings and work their way down to more ordinary vehicles. Barrett-Jackson, for example, starts with lower entry cars on Tuesday and Wednesday. Prime time is Thursday, Friday, and Saturday. Regardless of the day, all vehicles are carefully staged so that they crescendo to the sale of high-end cars.

## Mission Accomplished

If you are the successful bidder, hold up your bid card high so the crew can give your registration number to the clerk and mark it on the tag of the vehicle you just bought. If you have no other business to conduct, then this is the time to go to the cashier's area, turn in your paddle, and pay for your purchase. You will receive an itemized printout of all charges and taxes applicable to the sale.

## When Buying More than One Vehicle

Some auctions yield up multiple treasures that you simply must own. When you have successfully bid on the first vehicle, jot down the lot number and the hammer price. You will pay for your purchases when you have completed your business or at the end of the auction.

## Sold!

If you win the bid you are contractually obligated to pay for the item. You cannot change your mind after the bidding has ended. Under consumer law, there is no cooling off period at an auction. You can stop at any time during the bidding process, but once you hear "Sold!" and the auctioneer identifies you, that vehicle is yours.

## Bidding in Absentia

Even though you may be physically unable to be present for an auction, that doesn't mean you can't place a bid. There are several ways to participate, even if you happen to be out of the country on the day of the sale.

## Live Telephone Bids

Telephone bids are arranged in advance of the sale date by the staff. They may send you to the Bid Department or to Client Services to set up your call. If you plan to bid by telephone, it is generally done on a first-come, first-serve basis. Don't wait until the last minute to register. Not all vehicles may be eligible for telephone bidding; there is an expected minimum price value. Cars and trucks below that point are not included in telephone bidding.

There are forms to fill out in order to register and secure a telephone line. These forms ask for proof of identity, residence, telephone number, fax number, e-mail, credit, and/or debit information from your bank.

On the day of the sale, a staff member from the auction house will telephone you about five vehicles before your car arrives on the block. Once your vehicle is on stage, the staff member will talk you through the bidding and ask you at each stage if you wish to bid higher. This will continue until you are successful or until you choose to bow out.

## Absentee Telephone or Fax Bids

Auction houses accept absentee bids a.k.a. a "written bid," a "commission bid," and an "order bid" on your behalf. With your written permission, they will act, in your place, to secure a vehicle for you at the lowest possible price. You register by completing an absentee bid form. These are found in the sale catalog, in the showroom, or online. In addition to supplying proof of identity and residence as well as credit and debit information, indicate the maximum price you are willing to pay for a specified vehicle. The hammer price you write down will not include the buyer's premium, other applicable surcharges, or taxes.

You may not be permitted to bid below the reserve price, and your bid may be required to fit the incremental bidding pattern the auction house uses. A bid of $33,333 makes no sense, since the bid increments would be by $1000. An acceptable bid would be $32,000 or $34,000.

If you are unable to access a physical absentee bid form, you may telephone your bid through to the auction house. The staff member will fill out the form with you over the phone. However, written confirmation, either by courier, fax, or mail, must be received at least 24 hours before the start of the auction in order for your phone conversation to be validated. Should two or more absentee bids of equal value be received, the bid bearing the earliest time stamp gets the nod.

## Canceling or Amending an Absentee Bid

It is permissible to change the price you are willing to pay or even cancel an absentee bid. The cutoff point for doing so is 24 hours before the sale begins. This may be done on the phone, but written confirmation must follow within the time limits set.

## Online Absentee Bids

Some auction houses offer online absentee bidding. Follow the instructions on the Web site in order to participate in this manner. The sites are secure; personal and credit information is safe.

Specialized bidding may be available only to preferred clients with a proven track record. Inquire as to whether or not you may use these services.

## Emergency or Covering Bids

In the event that you are unreachable during the auction, an emergency or cover bid can be executed on your behalf. This is a pre-determined bid amount that a staff member is authorized to use, on behalf of a telephone bidder.

## Verification

An hour or so after the conclusion of the auction, it is your duty to call the auction house and determine whether or not your bid was the successful one. If you do not call, only the highest bidder will be advised of the purchase and then only by invoice.

## Getting Your Vehicle Home

Every auction has time limits for removal of sold vehicles from the auction site. It may be 24 hours, noon the next day, or 10 days. Find out what the house rules are ahead of time. Failure to take them away results in removal charges, storage fees, and taxes.

David Hansen elected to trailer home his 1912 Rambler Gotham Limousine from Wisconsin to his suburban Chicago home. (Photo courtesy of David Hansen and Jim Heide)

You cannot remove your vehicle from the premises until the auction house has approved your financial arrangements.

### Driving

Not all vehicles can be driven home from the auction site. If you are going to pilot your baby home, make sure you have a temporary transit permit and insurance coverage. You will also want to have tools in case it should break down along the way.

### Self-Trailering

Whether it's a flatbed trailer or enclosed, this is a safe way to get your vehicle home. Blankets or a car cover will protect the finish if you're using a flatbed trailer. Some jurisdictions no longer allow vehicles to be hauled by car dolly.

## Professional Delivery

A number of companies specialize in transporting collectible automobiles. A big auction house will have representatives from several of these companies on site. If you wish to use their services, shop beforehand so you know which one suits your particular needs. The transport company needs to be able to fit your time frame, too. If you live in Three Sheets, Wyoming, population 160, you may wait weeks before your vehicle is delivered. If you know of a shipper who has a depot near you, inquire if they will or can be at the show.

Some of the big names are Intercity Lines and FedEx Custom Critical Passport Auto Transport. Show the Bill of Lading to the cashier before paying for your wheels. This will permit the cashier to waive any applicable sales taxes if you are taking the car out of the state or province in which the auction was conducted.

## Advantages of Professional Delivery

Hauling vintage and classic cars is what these companies do every day. The vehicles they transport are fully insured during the trip. Your vehicle will be level-loaded into an enclosed trailer to prevent strain on the drivetrain and suspension. The better companies even have satellite tracking so your car's whereabouts are known at all times.

Having sung the praises of the professional cartage firms, it is important to remember that Mother Nature can always throw an unexpected monkey wrench into the delivery works. One December, Rhonda Gelstein fell in love with a 1959 AMC Metropolitan. She lives in a suburb of Detroit, and the car was in Connecticut. After extensive conversations and many photographs were e-mailed, Rhonda closed the deal. She would finally own her own Met. The certified check was overnighted by a courier company on December 22. A blizzard brought the entire Northeast to a standstill that night. Thousands of motorists were stranded on interstates. Schools were closed, too. In fact, entire towns were shut down. The courier flight with Rhonda's payment was grounded for several days and then the letter got lost. With time, citizens dug themselves out of the blizzard, but things like long distance car deliveries fell far behind. Finally everything got back to normal, and the Metropolitan arrived at its new home on January 11.

Savvy Tip

Transport companies ship when they have full loads. Your vehicle may be weeks away from arriving on your doorstep. It can be anticlimactic to have the car or truck delivered so long after the purchase. Fortunately the loads are tracked by satellite, so the whereabouts are known at all times.

# 12 TIME TO PAY UP

Auctions are good, clean fun for the whole family, provide more laughs and thrills than a barrelful of monkeys, and yes, they are great entertainment whether you watch or participate. We have also learned there are bargains to be had if one does one's homework and bids artfully. All this fun comes with a price tag. At auctions, there are several not-so-visible fees added to the final price after the hammer falls.

## Entrance Fees

Some auctions charge nothing to attend, although you will pay for the catalog. At others, you will be asked to make a donation. Entry fees can range from a few dollars up to several hundred. At a first-tier house event, you pay for the catalog and that serves as your entry ticket to the auction.

Make sure you have your catalog with you when you arrive at the auction event.

## Buyer's Premium

The final hammer price is never the amount that you will pay for your car. When it comes time to pay for your wheels, auction houses add a commission fee, or a buyer's premium, to the final bid. The fee varies widely depending on the firm. Do ask in advance so as not to be shocked when arriving at the cashier's counter.

## Currency

Sales are always conducted in and payment is made in the currency of the country in which the auction takes place. It costs two to three percent to convert from one currency to another. Shop around for the best exchange rate if you plan to attend an auction abroad. Sometimes you can do better purchasing currency outside of the country.

Most of the large firms display a large, easy-to-read currency conversion board throughout the proceedings. This is very helpful for clients who are not familiar with the currency being used or not quick at calculating the current bid into familiar home currency.

You may do well to pay for your purchase by credit card. Check with your credit card company. Some offer a preferential rate on foreign purchases, special deals or large purchases, or fees on this type of transaction.

## Taxes

Be prepared to pay all applicable taxes on your vehicle when you pay for it at the cashier's office. Purchasers who live outside the jurisdiction of the sale may have the sales taxes refunded by mail or have it waived on the spot. Some vehicles will be subject to a special excise tax or luxury taxes in the jurisdictions where they will be licensed. International purchasers may have to pay for an import or export license or need the services of a brokerage firm to get their babies home. The staff will inform you of your requirements and options, if you advise them of your circumstances.

A vehicle equipped with air-conditioning and registered anywhere in Canada is subject to the federal government's $100 luxury tax.

## Payment Terms

It's cash on the barrelhead for vehicles bought at an auction. Whether you pay by a pre-approved line of credit, write a check on your account, or flash a credit card, no vehicle leaves the area until it is paid for in full. The cashier will advise you as to when you may take your car or truck home.

## Letters of Credit

Buying a vintage car or truck will cost a pretty penny or two. Banks have a category of pleasure loans for customers wishing to purchase boats and planes, take a once-in-a-lifetime cruise, or acquire a heritage item such as a vintage car. The loan officer at your financial institution will arrange an appropriate line of credit and give you a letter of introduction to take to the auction with you. Some financial institutions charge a small fee for such a letter.

## Lines of Credit

Some of the prestige houses are equipped to arrange a line of credit for preferred customers through financial institutions of their choosing. The line of credit offered will be commensurate with your portfolio and will include a credit card. With this line of credit, you can always raise your paddle with confidence at the auction.

## Make Sure You Get What You Pay For

Ken Buttolph was editor of *The Standard Guide to Cars & Prices* for many years. He bought a 1940 Chevrolet at a major auction. He paid for his purchase and left the cashier's office to cover the rest of the auction. An hour later he was advised he had bought the wrong car, that he had actually purchased a 1947 Chevrolet. The house assured Ken that it was an honest mistake. The issue was resolved by drawing straws. He lost out and wound up with the car he didn't want. Later, a senior member of the auction house who had heard the story approached Ken. The official expressed anger at the overt scam. He told Ken that he had been railroaded, and it wouldn't happen again.

## Taking Possession

You have just purchased your dream wheels; the hammer has fallen. The ringman is with you. One of the clerks will approach you with a "buy ticket" printed in duplicate. This is a contract of sale with the lot number, vehicle description, and the purchase price written on it. It is signed immediately. Your copy goes in your pocket. The vehicle should be paid for by the end of the day but absolutely must be paid for by the end of the event.

Be patient when paying, there may be lines. You're not the only person to buy a vehicle at this auction. If there's a long line, purchasers' names all go on a list. Cashing out at an auction is just like waiting for a table in a good restaurant. To make the wait time more pleasant there may be refreshments on hand and comfortable places to sit. At a large event, there may be as many as a good dozen cashiers to process the sales.

If the paperwork is in order, the average auction transaction takes about 15 minutes per vehicle purchased. If you have bought multiple vehicles, the time with the cashier will be correspondingly longer. How long is a good question. One auction official sagely advises, "How long is a piece of string?"

When it's time to pay, make sure you have everything ready for the cashier. Bring a full measure of patience and good will, too. Purchasers who exhibit inappropriate behavior will be refused service and advised to return when they choose to be cooperative.

## Paperwork

When it is your turn to pay, you will be seated at a desk with a cashier who will pull out the appropriate dossier for the lot number you have purchased. In that file is the consigner's contract and proof of payment, the vehicle's description, the original title and a copy, and a document listing power of attorney signed by the seller—needed for the cashier to complete the sale. Also in the file will be the dealer's license, a detailed description, and photographs of the vehicle. If the car is purchased in the United States, there will be a report that verifies the odometer has not been rolled back and that all Federal Odometer Laws have been met, bills of sale, and approved bidders' applications. If the vehicle has a 17-digit VIN, it will have been run through CARFAX and that report included. Then, from the bidder department, the cashier will pull the bidder agreement. With these documents in hand, legal transfer of ownership to you can begin.

Race cars are required to be sold with specific disclaimers that the purchaser understands the vehicle is not legitimate for street use.

Race cars, like this 1968 AMX, when sold at auctions have accompanying paperwork that must be signed. The new owner acknowledges the vehicle is not street legal.

Once the deal is complete the sale file is kept on hand for mandatory future audits by the Department or Ministry of Motor Vehicles.

## Payment

The process of settling up with the auction house is very similar to buying a vehicle at any car dealership. This is the point where the cashier is ready to take your money. Payment is by wire transfer, cash, or a check. Some of the larger houses accept pre-approved credit cards. Under no circumstances will the vehicle be going home with you until the money has changed hands.

Vehicles not paid for by the end of the show will be placed in storage and fees charged.

Keep your bank's phone number handy! If you should go over the approved line of credit issued from your financial institution, the situation must be resolved immediately. A new line of credit will have to be authorized by the bank and verified in writing.

## Shipping Paperwork

Prior to cashing out, the paperwork for shipment and delivery must be in hand, so that the cashier knows what taxes to collect. If you do not live in the jurisdiction where the auction took place, you will sign a form that the car is leaving that state or province. This keeps you from paying taxes that could take months to collect back from the revenue agency.

Savvy Tip

Driving your own wheels away from the auction means that you will pay the taxes in the jurisdiction of the sale. To avoid paying the tax, the vehicle must leave the auction site courtesy of a carrier licensed by the Interstate Commerce Commission or the Ministry of Transport. The only exception to this law is dealers.

## Wire Transfers

No vehicle is released until the wire transfer is received from the bank by the auction house. It can take 24 hours or longer for one to come in. After the last "i" is dotted and the last "t" is crossed, a car release is given. The car release must then be presented to the carrier if the vehicle is to be hauled. Because of the convenience, the vast majority of vehicles purchased at the large auction events leave by carrier.

# 13 THIS IS THE LAW

Consumer law varies greatly throughout the United States, its territories, and possessions. The same is true in each of the 10 provinces of Canada and its territories. As a wise shopper, you will want to familiarize yourself with the facts and laws as they pertain to you in the jurisdiction where you live and the jurisdiction where you will purchase your vehicle. If you are from Texas and you purchase a vehicle in Vancouver, you must know what the laws are in British Columbia. We all know that Texas is big, but laws from the Lone Star State do not apply to transactions made in Canada. It falls on you to know what each party is legally liable for in the completion of a transaction.

At auctions, as in any other consumer transaction, the rule is always "buyer beware." Although a Niagara of legislation has been enacted to protect consumers, the shopper steps outside of that circle of safety when participating in an auction. The auction house serves as a middleman or a broker, working on behalf of the seller to provide the buyer with the opportunity to purchase.

The auction house takes vehicles on consignment and works with the information the seller provides. Though it does its best, the staff at an auction house does not have the means or resources to verify every fact and prove the condition of each vehicle that will cross the block on the day of the event. Due diligence is the legal term for doing your homework and that falls squarely on you, the buyer.

"Sold as is" means exactly what it says. Verbal promises made to you by the owner mean nothing in a court of law. There is no warranty; there is no guarantee unless you have gotten the owner to put any and all promises in writing. The deal is irrevocable according to the laws of the land when the hammer falls and the auctioneer shouts "Sold!"

The 1960 Rambler was the fourth best selling car in the United States and held the Lucky Thirteen Spot in Canada.

Dad always used to say that before you get into an agreement, know how to get out of it gracefully. His wise advice goes a long way toward preserving good friendships and protecting any two parties who do business together.

Before you register at an auction, find out how the auction house arbitrates disputes in the event that it is necessary to do so after a sale.

## Follow Your Instincts

If you have a bad feeling about a vehicle, follow your gut feeling and walk away from it. No matter how badly you want that car or truck, first impressions are so often the right ones. Chances are the example you're standing in front of is not the last one on the planet. Save yourself a lot of grief, anguish, and expense down the road. If your sixth sense tells you "no," then by all means go have a cup of coffee, think about it, and cool off. You can come back later or continue the hunt another day.

The auction house will have a bill of sale, proof of lien searches, and paperwork for any court orders, if such are applicable to the vehicle you wish to purchase. Be sure to ask for them.

## The Title

Buying a car with the title listed as being "In Transit" can be a very dubious proposition. If all the paperwork isn't on hand at the time of the sale, don't buy. You've parted with your cash, paid the auction house in full, and they in turn will pay the seller, but you haven't received your full due. If you do decide to buy the vehicle anyway, make sure the sales contract stipulates the maximum length of time that will pass before you receive the title. If it takes longer, the seller is in breach of contract. Demand and get a full refund. It can take months to get a title cleared, and it is possible you may never get one at all.

Canadian vehicles don't come with titles. The registration doubles as the title, streamlining the sales process. Once the owner signs off on the registration form, the vehicle is yours.

## Failure to Disclose

It can happen that the owner has not made full disclosure about the automobile's condition to the auction house. This can constitute breach of contract. This is particularly true if the car has been written off because it has been totaled in an accident or written off after a fire or flood.

## Stolen Vehicles

Should the car turn out to be stolen property, there is legal recourse. A forged or falsified title or registration also invalidates the sale. I knew a man who bought a sweet 1960 Rambler station wagon that turned out to be stolen. Several months after he purchased his pride and joy, police seized the car. The seller was long gone and the unhappy customer wound up going to court to get his money back from the auction company.

### Clones

Sometimes ordinary, run-of-the-mill automobiles are upgraded into a more desirable model. These are called clones and have reached such a proportion in the antique auto auction world that they have become legitimately desirable purchases. As long as the clone is properly identified, all is well. It can happen that an unscrupulous owner may attempt to pass off a clone as the real deal and that is fraudulent.

A clone is only a legitimate vehicle when it is properly identified and placed on the block as the knock-off that it is.

### Shill Bidding

Shill bidding is when the seller or someone in association with the seller plants a phony bidder in the crowd who is there only to push up the price. The shill has no intention whatsoever of buying the vehicle on the block. None of the other bidders are wise to the situation and continue to bid in good faith. When there is a false bidder in the crowd, this constitutes fraud.

## An Ounce of Prevention

Oh, it is so true that an ounce of prevention is worth a pound of cure. While it is easy enough to sue, the time and trouble will wear on your nerves. No matter what else it does, it will diminish greatly any joy that you might get from the vehicle you have purchased. You may even grow to hate the car altogether because of the problems it represents. It is much wiser to take the time to study the proposition carefully and get what you want and need in writing.

With a good understanding of the law, you certainly will be wise enough to avoid the common pitfalls and dangers that could potentially ruin a purchase experience.

Hopefully the things you have learned throughout this book have been helpful in introducing you to the auction world, or if you are a seasoned veteran, it has helped to sharpen your skills as a consumer at an auction.

# APPENDIX

## Glossary of Auction Terms

(As they pertain to vintage automobile auctions)

**Absentee Bid:** A client's instructions directing the auction house to bid on one or more vehicles up to the maximum amount the client has specified for each vehicle. Absentee bids are also called written bids, commission bids, and order bids.

**Auction:** A public sale where vintage automobiles are sold to bidders.

**Auction Estimate:** The amount of cash a vehicle may sell for at auction as determined by the auction house.

**Auctioneer:** The person who conducts an auction. The auctioneer introduces each vehicle offered for sale and acknowledges bids, the final bid prices, and the paddle numbers of successful bidders.

**Auctioneer's Book:** This is the legal record of the auction with paddle numbers of successful bidders and final bid prices for each vehicle.

**Bid:** The current offer for a specific vehicle.

**Bid Clerk**: See "sale clerk."

**Bidder:** One of many individuals offering to purchase a vehicle at auction.

**Block:** The podium or sale area where the current vehicle is being sold during an auction.

**Buyer's Premium:** A surcharge added to the final hammer price the buyer pays to the auction house.

**Catalog:** An illustrated record of the vehicles offered for sale in a particular auction.

**Client Number:** The unique number assigned by an auction house to a particular client to expedite business transactions with that client.

**Condition Report:** A written description of the vehicle's condition prepared as an extra cost service either by the auction house staff or an agent acting on behalf of the auction house to prospective bidders upon request.

**Conditions of Sale/Conditions of Business:** Legal limits that govern the purchase of vehicles.

**Conversion Board:** An electronic display board that displays bid amounts in several currencies.

**Final Bid Price:** See "hammer price."

**Hammer Price:** The final bid price as announced by the auctioneer when the gavel falls. This price does not include the buyer's premium.

**Increments:** Regular amounts of money the auctioneer uses to raise bidding.

**Order Bid:** See "absentee bid."

**Paddle:** A numbered plastic card assigned to identify a particular bidder registered for an auction. The paddle is raised to indicate a bid. The auctioneer calls out the paddle number of the successful bidder as each vehicle is sold.

**Pass:** A term used when the bidding for a vehicle does not reach its reserve price.

**Preview:** See "viewing."

**Price Realized:** The actual amount of money or the purchase price to be paid by the successful bidder. It includes the hammer price plus the buyer's premium, any surcharges, and all taxes.

**Real Money:** The amount the successful bidder will lay down for a purchase before in-house charges and taxes are applied.

**Ringman:** See "sale clerk."

**Reserve Price:** The lowest amount a vehicle may sell for placed on the car by the owner. If the vehicle does not meet the reserve price, it is moved off the block as a "no sale."

**Sale Clerk:** The staff member who assists the auctioneer in spotting bidders, recording successful amounts and paddle numbers, and executing absentee bids. Also called a bid clerk and a ringman.

**Telephone Bid:** A bid made through a staff member who telephones a client from the saleroom then relays the client's bid on a particular vehicle to the auctioneer during the vehicle's exposure to bidding.

**Viewing:** An exhibition of vehicles to be offered for sale held in advance of the auction. Also called previews or exhibitions.

## Glossary of Collectible Vehicle Terms

**AACA:** Antique Automobile Club of America.

**Antique:** A vehicle that is eligible for historic status, usually at 25 years of age, though some states and provinces will grant special license and special plates for vehicles that are 20 years old.

**B-Pillar:** An automotive design term describing the vertical post that separates the front and rear side windows on a coupe, two-door sedan, four-door sedan, and a station wagon. Convertibles and hardtop convertibles eliminate this feature.

**Blueprinted Engine:** An engine that has been rebuilt and tuned to original factory specifications.

**Build Sheet:** The physical piece of paper that accompanied a vehicle down the factory lines during assembly. This paper lists all the components and options ordered and built into the car, the date of manufacture of the body and engine, the date of completion, and the date of shipment to the initial distributor or dealer.

**Build Tag:** A metal (on newer vehicles it is plastic) tag affixed to the body with a record of the chassis, body, paint code, and engine's serial numbers.

**CCCA:** Classic Car Club of America.

**Classic Car**: Certain luxury cars generally built in limited numbers usually between the years of 1925 and 1948. These cars are designated as "classic" by the CCCA.

**Collector Car or Collectible Car:** Any vehicle that a potential buyer or owner deems worth collecting.

**Condition Scales:** Rating systems used to establish a vehicle's physical shape and value.

**Elcometer:** A digital device that measures paint thickness and body filler on a vehicle.

**Frame-off Restoration:** This term means that literally every piece of the machine has been disassembled, taken off the frame, and restored to "like new" condition before being rebuilt. The expression applies equally to Unibody vehicles manufactured without frames.

**Hardtop:** Originally called a "hardtop convertible." Even though the steel top is fixed in place, this is a car that has no B-pillar.

**Limited Edition:** Cars or trucks intentionally built in very small numbers.

**MCS:** Milestone Car Society.

**Matching Numbers:** An indication that the vehicle is completely original. The chassis, body, paint code, and engine serial numbers all match the build tag on the vehicle.

**Milestone Car:** This is a vehicle that has special status among vintage car collectors. Eligibility of a vehicle for this designation is established by the Milestone Car Society.

**Monocoque:** See "unibody."

**Parts Exchange Books:** Lists that show what parts will interchange from one automobile or truck to another.

**Unibody or Unit Body:** Also called monocoque construction, this is a vehicle built without a separate frame.

**VCCA:** Vintage Car Club of America.

**VIN:** Vehicle Identification Number.

**Vintage Car**: A vehicle that is 25 years or older but has not been accorded classic status.

**Working Girl:** A collectible car or truck that is an integral part of one's business, earns significant income, or is a valid tax deduction for the owner.

# INDEX

# C



# D



# E



# F

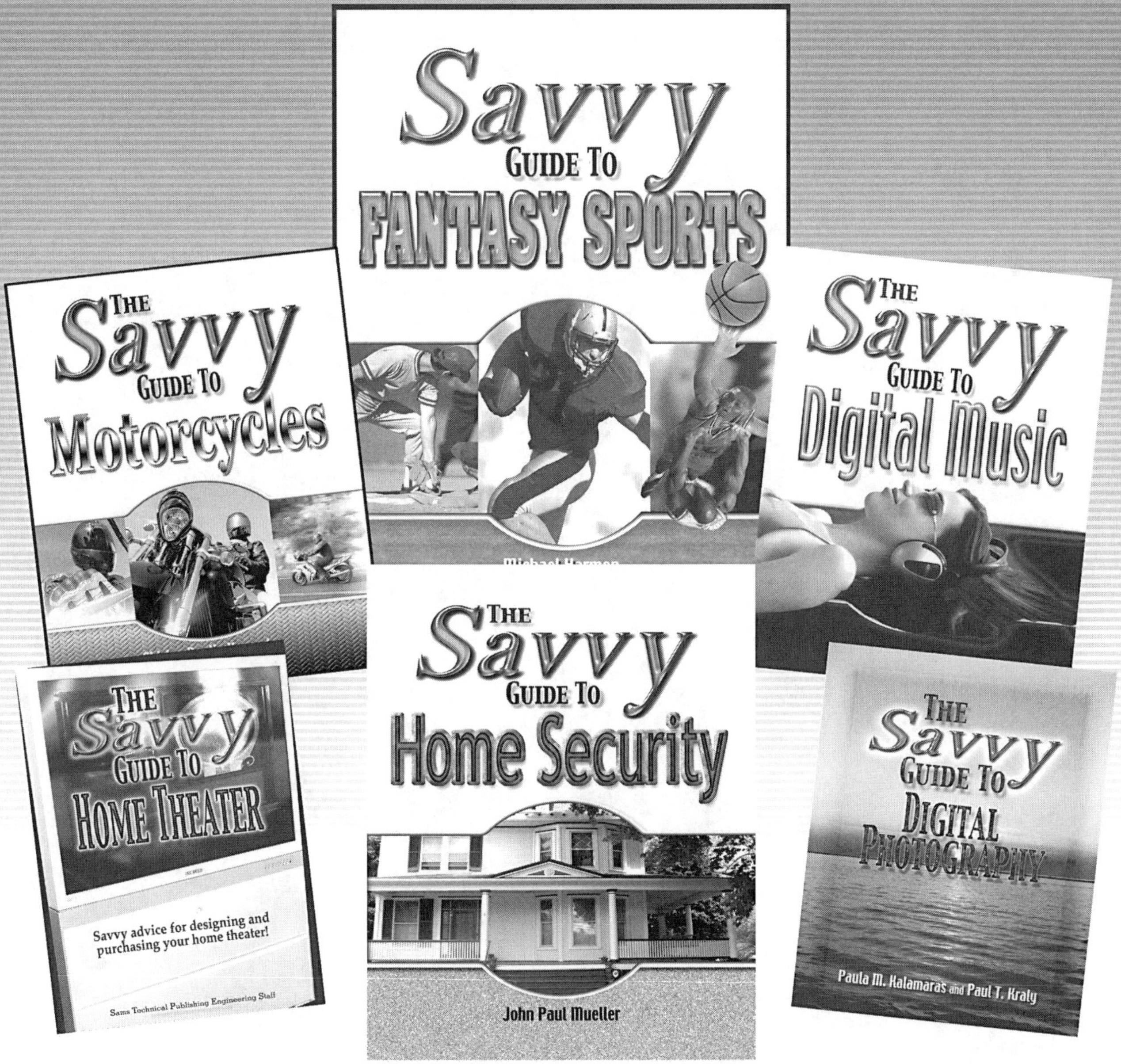

Available at your local bookseller or online retailer.